THE
SCOTS
KIRK

Cover Picture
Etching of early St. Andrew's complete with horse sheds.
Note that the artist, Jack Martin, labelled the picture *St. Andrew's, Bendale.*

THE SCOTS KIRK

(Known by some as the "Scotch" Church)

AN ORAL HISTORY OF
ST. ANDREW'S PRESBYTERIAN CHURCH,
SCARBOROUGH

Andrew Chadwick, Bruce McCowan
& Nancy McCowan
with Committee Assistance

*A St. Andrew's Scarborough
Bicentennial Project*

NATURAL HERITAGE / NATURAL HISTORY INC.

Copyright © 1997 St. Andrew's Presbyterian Church, Scarborough

All rights reserved. No portion of this book, with the exception of brief extracts for the purpose of literary review, may be reproduced in any form without the permission of the publisher.

Published by Natural Heritage / Natural History Inc. (P.O. Box 95, Station O, Toronto, Ontario M4A 2M8) for the Kirk Session of St. Andrew's Presbyterian Church, Scarborough, Ontario M1P 4N2.

First edition

Canadian Cataloguing in Publication Data

Chadwick, Andrew, 1968-
    The Scots Kirk

Includes bibliographical references and index.

ISBN 1-896219-26-8

1. St. Andrew's Presbyterian Church (Scarborough, Ont.) – History. I. McCowan, Bruce. II. McCowan, Nancy. III. Title

BX9215.S39C43 1997   285'.2713541   C97-931293-0

Design by Heather Keith

Printed and bound in Canada by Hignell Printing, Winnipeg, Manitoba

"For all the Saints!"

This book is dedicated to the memory of those who have gone before us in the faith in this historic church.

In particular, we are thankful for the life of Bessie Irene Laurie, whose generous bequest helped to fund the production of this book.

PREFACE

History has been defined as "the essence of innumerable biographies." In other words, history is about people -- their activities, thoughts, ambitions and disappointments -- and this history of St. Andrew's Presbyterian Church, Scarborough, certainly fits that description. It is a book about people.

Traditionally congregational histories have been based on documentary evidence such as minutes of Sessions, Boards and affiliated groups like social clubs, Ladies' Aid, Sunday School or the Scouting movement. Oral history as used here may seem like a new source of information for writing history, but in fact it is very ancient. Most books of the Bible, for instance, written years after the happenings they recount, were based on oral traditions preserved by older generations.

This volume has been drawn almost exclusively from oral history. Some selections describe incidents long past, others tell of activities that are almost contemporary. Its rainbow of reminiscences touches on the material structure of St. Andrew's, on worship and music, on youth work and social happenings, on individuals who built this congregation and on just plain fun events. Happily, in the hands of the several authors, nostalgia has been tempered by realism.

We are indebted to many for this interesting and readable collection of annals and anecdotes about St. Andrew's congregation and I personally hope it is not the end of this bicentennial project. Between the covers of this book there is both encouragement and invitation to undertake other histories of St. Andrew's, from more and different viewpoints and from other types of records. May the present volume also point to the importance of making and preserving full and permanent records of this historic congregation, for the benefit of future generations.

John S. Moir, M.A., PH.D., D.D.
Emeritus Professor of History, University of Toronto
Sessional Lecturer in Canadian Presbyterian History,
Knox College

GENERAL INTRODUCTION & ACKNOWLEDGMENTS

This history of St. Andrew's, Scarborough, began with an Oral History Project organized by the James McCowan Memorial Social History Society, a non-profit, non-charitable organization interested in preserving our Scottish heritage. The ultimate goal was to produce an Oral History book to commemorate St. Andrew's 175th Anniversary.

Andrew Chadwick and Michael Morrow, two recent history graduates of Scarborough College, University of Toronto, eagerly began to interview a number of members and past members of the congregation. Nancy McCowan assembled and typed almost two hundred pages of additional oral history anecdotes and extracts from old Treasurer's Reports.

With the approval of Session, a committee comprised of six interested St. Andrew's people -- Wayne Armstrong, Christine Ferguson, Heather Keith, Janet F. Main, Nancy McCowan and Bruce McCowan -- assisted by volunteer Andrew Chadwick, began the process of putting the book together. Part One, "A Selected Social History", was composed by Andrew Chadwick. Part Two, "The Physical Property", was compiled by Nancy McCowan and Bruce McCowan. Neither Part would have been possible without the valuable story contributions of many -- too numerous to mention here lest we miss one. Janet F. Main assisted with the editing, Wayne Armstrong cared for and organized the photographs, and Heather Keith typed the final text. The Committee is particularly grateful to Professor John Moir who kindly contributed the Preface, and to Dr. John A. Johnston who thoughtfully wrote an Afterword. These gentlemen are two of the most learned of Presbyterian Church historians.

True to the original intent, this book is, for the most part, an oral history. Data from written records has been added to supplement the verbal testimony and to take the story back to St. Andrew's humble backwoods origins in 1818. The 1975 book, "St. Andrew's Presbyterian Church", by the late Jenny McCowan, was a valuable source of information, particularly with respect to the pre-war photographs. A bibliography is provided.

In a predominantly oral history study such as this, endnotes make little contribution. To a small degree, we have attempted a "values" approach to this book -- hence, the reader will not detect a chronological pattern, but rather subject themes reflecting the values of the people.

Now, in 1997, this book is being published as one of several of St. Andrew's Scarborough Bicentennial Projects. Official Township celebrations in 1896 and 1946 to commemorate the Centennial and Sesquicentennial were held at St. Andrew's. So, it is only fitting that St. Andrew's should make a lasting contribution to the Two Hundredth Anniversary of

Scarborough's modern-age settlement. St. Andrew's other Bicentennial Projects included: the stage production "Grin and Board It" on April 13; a "Kirkin' O' The Tartan" on July 7; and a Cemetery Memorial Service and re-dedication of the David and Mary Thomson Memorial on July 14, 1996.

Thanks are due to the many who contributed their memories to this project. Well over one hundred photographs were received. As one can imagine, enough material was assembled to prepare several large volumes. Decisions on what to exclude from the finished product proved very difficult to make. Perhaps in the future supplements could be published so that gaps in the St. Andrew's story will, over time, be at least partially filled.

Of course, a final chapter can never be written. The legacy that has been left by the thousands who have made St. Andrew's Scarborough one of Ontario's longest-living Scottish social institutions will be interpreted and re-interpreted for as long as people care about people.

Bruce McCowan, Co-Chairman
James McCowan Memorial Social History Society

Many Thanks to those who contributed illustrations for this book

Wayne Armstrong
Dorothy Brown
Mary Cameron
Rev. Catherine Chalin
Agnes Conkey
Rev. Joyce Davis
Alex Fernie
Betty Hawthorne
Daphne Kaye
Charlene Lyn

Trevor Lyn
Janet Main
Doris McAndless
Bob McCowan
Nancy McCowan
Walter McCowan
Myrnie Venn
Carol Wright
St. Andrew's Collection

"St. Andrew's Presbyterian Church: A History from 1818"

St. Andrew's Church Lane looking west

TABLE OF CONTENTS

PART I - A Selected Social History
Andrew Chadwick

	Page
The Women's Missionary Society & The Presbyterian Women	1
Young People's Society	10
The Choir	12
The '39 Club	21
Ninth Toronto Boys' Brigade	22
The Couples' Club	26
The Bell Choirs - 1992	29
A Wedding at St. Andrew's, 1956	30
Easter Eggs - 1961-62	33
Covenanters' Service, 1974	34
Robbie Burns Suppers	35
Ministers	38
A Few St. Andrew's Families	46
Boat People	49
Thomas Gibson - 1924	51
The Andrews	52
The Scotts	53
Janet Taylor Purdie McCowan	54
Reminiscences of Long-Time St. Andrew's Members	56

Selected Illustrations (1840 - 1996)   69 - 92

TABLE OF CONTENTS

PART II - The Physical Property
Compiled by Bruce McCowan & Nancy Weir McCowan

	Page
Introduction	95
Maintenance & Operation - Treasurer's Books	101
The Architecture of St. Andrew's Sanctuary	105
Boys Will Be Boys!	110
Renovation and Restoration, 1990	111
Memorial Stained Glass Windows	116
Steeple Restoration, 1992	119
A Progressive Recycling Society	122
The Original Frame Church	122
The "Old" Manse, 1853	123
The Minister's Driving Shed	128
The Horse Sheds	131
The White Sunday School Building	133
The Christian Education Building, 1957	135
Break & Enter	141
The Kirkyard	141
Coincidence or Fate? A Poem from 1894	145
The Cemetery Controversy	147
Caretakers and the Sexton's House	149
Ewart & Della Gray & The Wee House at St. Andrew's Cemetery	152
The Glebe	150
Scarboro' Centennial Memorial Library	155
St. Andrew's Subdivision & The Library	156
The Story of St. Andrews Road	157
Concluding Remarks	159
Afterword	160
Further Reading	161
Index	163

INTRODUCTION TO PART I

When I first agreed to co-write a history of St. Andrew's Presbyterian Church, I really didn't know anything about the congregation. I was the only one involved in the project without ties to the church and I had a lot to learn.

What I discovered during the past few years is not something wholly original or dramatic but that should not diminish its importance. The men and women who have been a part of the St. Andrew's family have much to be proud of, both as Christians and as members of the local community. Their hard work and devotion to ideals have done much for the growth of Scarborough. This is the legacy of St. Andrew's and I am proud to be your guide.

Two people who were instrumental in getting this project finished should get special mention. First and foremost, I would like to thank Nancy McCowan. Without her tireless work in collecting stories and getting others to participate, the project would be a mere shell of its current state. Finally, I would also like to mention Janet F. Main. Janet took my work, questionable use of grammar and all, and she pulled it into a cohesive and enjoyable whole. These two ladies made my job a lot easier.

Andrew Chadwick
Honours B.A. in History
University of Toronto

PART I

THE WOMEN'S MISSIONARY SOCIETY & THE PRESBYTERIAN WOMEN

Churches are, first and foremost, places where people of a particular faith can demonstrate and develop their religion. This notion, while true in a very narrow sense, does not take into account the essential social function that churches have served in their communities. The many different distractions the contemporary world presents have altered this role somewhat. Some would argue that a modern world has no need for these anachronistic institutions; simply put, "we've outgrown them." In response to this, we can offer up the example of St. Andrew's, whose clubs have evolved over the years from a necessary social outlet for an isolated farm community to a socially responsible arm of the district. The different associations that have been a hallmark of St. Andrew's since its inception have always been relevant to the life of Scarborough. The tracing of this history can help show us much about how the role of churches in general has developed.

One of the most illustrious and long-standing associations of St. Andrew's has been the Women's Missionary Society in all its different forms. In 1856, it was first known as the Female Juvenile Association and, by all accounts, the first meeting may have taken place on December 22, 1856. We cannot be sure of the accuracy of this reference, for it appears in only one book and it is untitled.

At this meeting, it was decided that they would form a Female Juvenile Association to promote female education in India and that, as part of this goal, they would sponsor a young orphan girl. To this end, the ladies soon found a proper candidate from a Calcutta orphanage and she was named Mary Thomson Scarboro. This experience apparently worked quite well for they soon adopted a second girl whose name became Margaret Bain.

To augment the amounts of money that the members themselves actually gave, the association decided to put a donation box in the church. Six months later, on July 6th, they opened the box to find 2 pounds, 6 shillings and 7 pence. This money was then sent to the Canadian School in Calcutta to help the different orphans the women had adopted. In ensuing years the process continued and grew, as other groups, such as the Jewish Mission for India and Mr. Epstein's Medicine Chest, benefitted from the generosity of St. Andrew's as well.

The Female Juvenile Association continued to operate for many years. However at some point the name changed to the Zenana Mission. Later still, in 1889, it merged with the Foreign Mission Society. Information about these changes is very sketchy, but it seems that the sponsorship of orphans and the education about missions in general continued. In fact the stories inspired one woman, Miss Harriet Thomson, to travel to India to work as a missionary in 1896. The name of the organization may have changed, but the process went on just the same.

In 1906 the younger ladies of St. Andrew's formed a new association known as the Women's (Home) Mission Society. This group was to concentrate on charity work within Canada. Membership fees were 25 cents a year and the members met in St. Andrew's White Sunday School building. The first President was Mrs. Beebe Carnaghan and her Vice-President was Miss Bella Walton.

This newer group was very active indeed. Much of their time was spent conducting quilting bees. This would first involve a special collection to obtain money for linings and thread. Once purchased, the materials would be handed out to the women to work their talents. In her memoirs, Mrs. Margaret Oldham recalled that when she was a member of the association, the *bees* would be conducted throughout the winter on the second Wednesday of every month. Sometimes when money and materials were scarce, Mrs. Oldham remembered, the quilts would be made out of old socks and dresses. You wouldn't know it though; the finished products were often quite warm and beautiful. Once finished the quilts were sent into the city to a central Presbyterian organization that sent the work out west to British Columbia, the Yukon and to Northern Ontario. At other times the work done at these bees was actually meant for the needy people of Toronto. Each church had to do its part in providing goods for what was referred to as a *bale*. The size of the *bale* would be determined by the size of the congregation.

The actual meetings were very formal and they were held in one of the ladies' homes or in the Sunday School building. The format ran like this: a call to worship, devotional with bible reading and meditation, singing of hymns and a prayer, and minutes of the previous meeting were read back. This was followed by a roll call that would be answered with a special verse or Scripture that pertained to the evening's topic of study. After this came the treasurer's report, other business and often a solo that pertained to a study on a country as outlined by the Women's Missionary Society (W.M.S.) of Canada. To finish up the evening the group would sing a hymn and close in prayer.

The members had the opportunity to explore many areas of the world such as: Japan, Tibet, Africa, South America, Formosa, Southeast Asia, The Holy Land and Taiwan. Dorothy Brown recalls many topics from the 1960's era, including "Koreans in Japan", "Women of the Bible", "Mission on our Doorstep", "Call to Witness", "World Food Crisis" and "Missions on the Street Where We Live". It is interesting to note that sometimes these discussions could get rather political for their time. In 1920 we have notes about some rather intriguing discussions concerning the push for more women medical missionaries. This evolved into a more particular discussion about the difficulties young women encountered in simply attending medical school. This further illustrates the point that the subjects encountered were often quite socially relevant and provided the women with much information and discussion material.

Records indicate that the ladies not only talked about helping the unfortunate, they certainly did their share. In 1911 the Society learned about the lonely conditions in which men in mining and lumber camps lived. In response they sent bags containing note paper, post cards, stamps and pencils. During the First World War, Christmas boxes were sent to St. Andrew's "boys" serving overseas. In 1919 the missionary, Ethel Glendenning, wrote back from India to the ladies, thanking them for their financial support towards building a girls' school in that country.

With the advent of Church Union in 1925 the W.M.S. had to reorganize its auxiliary. In April it was requested that an announcement be made from the pulpit "...in reference to certain changes to be made in society." It was moved by Mrs. A. Stirling that the current auxiliary, as it stood within the old church hierarchy, be disbanded. The newly constituted auxiliary began its work in May, but the change seems to have been only in terms of organization, for the ladies' work continued in the same manner as before.

In May of 1954, a separate organization, known as the Women's Association, was formed. The purpose of the new group was to help the Board of Managers with the upkeep of the church by various money-raising activities and also to provide fellowship among the women of St. Andrew's. The first President was Mrs. Kathleen Gibson and the first Vice-President was Mrs. Carol Wright.

By 1958 the club had been joined by a group from the St. Andrew's Gardens subdivision. The two met under a joint executive. This leadership held meetings four times a year in March, June, September and December, while the two groups named Alpha and Friendship met every month. In 1959 these two groups were re-divided into five, with a chairperson heading each.

Mrs. Dorothy Brown has spent many years as a member of St. Andrew's and she remarked upon the charity of the ladies, both within the club and in the community. She writes, "The love and concern for the group was evidenced in the sending to members appropriate cards, such as get well, new baby, and sympathy, or flowers, plants, or fruit on suitable occasions. Layettes for Evangel Hall, Christmas hampers for the needy, and stamps for the Leprosy Mission were other worthy projects."

Eventually the group went back to two groups, an evening and an afternoon session. The afternoon group would concentrate on missions around the world and learning about the various cultures that they would contact.

The evening group would pay attention to the needs of those closer to home, namely the congregation of St. Andrew's.

By 1969, the clubs had amalgamated for one final time as they became known as Presbyterian Women. A list of their accomplishments in the years that followed demonstrates that the new association kept up the fine tradition of all its forebears. Examples include raising money for many projects such as new carpeting and curtains for the church in 1971. In 1973, by saving old Dominion Grocery Store cash register tapes, the ladies were able to purchase pots for the kitchen. Today, the organization is always front-and-centre when the congregation needs it most.

Raising money by organizing different events and catering services are important, but, as we have seen, the modern Presbyterian Women's group owes its roots to those who would help others both at home and beyond. This process has continued at St. Andrew's back from the earliest days of the W.M.S.. In 1964 this was evident when the decision was made to sponsor a child in India. In 1988 the newest in a long line of sponsored children was six-year-old Emmanuel Wanammuno, who lived with relatives in Kampala, Uganda. The names of the associations may change, but the good works continue. Time and again the women's groups of St. Andrew's have been an excellent example of organization, determination, and Christian charity. As you can see, the ladies of St. Andrew's today are certainly maintaining the high standards of their sisters who preceded them.

A group of St. Andrew's ladies (probably c. 1900)

Group of W.M.S. ladies in front of White Sunday School Hall. (c. 1910-11)

Group of W.M.S. ladies in front of White Sunday School Hall. (c. 1910-11)

Members of the Women's Missionary Society (1940's)
Back Row L-R Mrs. Betty (Thomas) Hawthorne, Mrs. A.D. Thomson, Mrs. Booth (Minister's housekeeper), Mrs. Alice (Arthur) Thomson,
Mrs. Florence (Ashley) McCowan, Miss Mary Thomson, Mrs. Forsythe, Mrs. Belle (D.J.) Davidson, Mrs. Jean (Arnold) Thomson
Mrs. Janet (Harold) McCowan, Mrs. Mary (William) Cameron,
Mrs. Mary Ann (Reith) (Levi) Chester, Olive Chester.
Front Row L-R Miss Abby Thomson, Mrs. Amy (Edward) Oldham, Mrs. Lil (Robert) Ormerod, Mrs. Maggie Bella (Wm.) McKean
Mrs. Mary (Frank) Weir, Mrs. Florence (Arch) Muir, Mrs. Ella (Harold) Hunter, Unknown, Mrs. Edith (Green) Walton

Women's Missionary Society and Friends (1940's)
Back Row - *Harold Hunter, Harold McCowan, Arnold Thomson, Andrew Fleming, Tom Hawthorne, Dr. D.J. Davidson*
Row 3 - *Ashley McCowan, Dr. Arthur Thomson, Florence McCowan, Edy Walton, Eleanor Weir, Marjorie Weir, Ella Hunter, Alice Thomson, Joyce Thomson, Belle Davidson, Mrs. Booth, Jean (Hunter) Forsythe, Janet McCowan, Jean Thomson, Mrs. Forsythe, Pearl Armstrong, Olive Chester, -----, Betty Hawthorne, Mary Cameron, Mrs. A.D. (Mary Larway) Thomson, Miss Mary Thomson, Mrs. Levi (Mary Ann Reith) Chester*
Row 2 - *Miss Abby (Abigail) Thomson, Mrs. Amy Oldham, Lil (Purdie) Ormerod, Maggie Bella (Thomson) McKean, Frank Weir, Florence Muir, Mary Weir, -----, Rev. J.W. Stephenson. --- Lyons, -----*
Front Row Children - *-----, Tom Armstrong, Bev Armstrong, Peg Forsythe, --- Lyons, --- Lyons*

Centennial Pageant of the Women's Missionary Society, 1967
Left to Right - *Mrs. Janet (Purdie) McCowan, Miss Elizabeth Stirling, Miss May Gardiner, Mrs. Marion (Thomson) McCowan, Mrs. Betty (Anderson) Hawthorne, Miss Margaret Stirling, Mrs. Jean (Ormerod) Thomson, Mrs. Margaret (Carmichael) Oldham.*

Some Ladies of St. Andrew's Women's Association, 1969
Back Row, L-R - *Mary Cowan, Daphne Kaye, Noelle Thomson, Virginia Sinclair*
Third Row, L-R - *Mary Cameron, Dorothy Brown, Christine Ferguson, Terry Fox*
Second Row, L-R - *Norean Cox, Marion McCowan, Kathleen MacNeill, Nancy McCowan*
Front Row, L-R - *Joyce Marks, Janet McCowan, Laura Watt, Mary Robertson, Betty Hawthorne, Mary MacQueen, Frances Brown*

YOUNG PEOPLE'S SOCIETY

An important part of any vibrant church community at the turn of the century was some sort of organization for the youth. Too young to participate in many of the organizations geared toward adults, the young people needed a group that could serve to educate them and to involve them in the Church as a whole. This is the void that the Young People's Society sought to fill.

Rev. D.B. MacDonald, the sixth minister of St. Andrew's, realized that the young people of his congregation would benefit greatly from a peer group to study their faith and to socialize as well. In 1897 the Young People's Society had its beginning. Leadership was provided by the minister with the help of the Society's President, Secretary, Treasurer and a Program Committee comprised of three or four other members. The group met each Sunday evening for their own service and every second week they had a "fun night", usually on a Wednesday.

When the group met for service one person led the evening, but everyone was encouraged to participate, as the purpose of the group was to develop fellowship among the young people. With over ninety persons at one time, this group was important in leading the young people to a better understanding of the spiritual aspects of St. Andrew's. An examination of the minute book for the Society shows the different topics that the group found relevant. For example, the meeting of November 30, 1904, featured a discussion of the topic, "How Intemperance Hinders Missions". Other meetings saw the group investigate "Birds and Flowers", "Temperance Organizations", and also "How to Break Bad Habits and Cultivate Good Ones".

These Sunday night meetings were important to the spiritual growth of St. Andrew's, but if you talk to anyone who was a member of the Society, they will probably lean back, smile, and tell you about the social evenings.

The importance of the bi-weekly socials becomes clearer when one realizes the kind of world in which these young men and women lived. In the early 1900's, there were no televisions or movie theatres to entertain people and, because it was a farming community, their closest friends were probably quite a distance away. The organized socials, therefore, were greatly welcomed.

A typical evening for the club might involve a singsong, croquinole and a discussion of some topic from the Bible. One restriction of note was card playing, for this was felt to be improper at a church gathering. The society even had its own newsletter, *The Echo*, whose editors included Velma Empringham, Ethel Coathup and Allan Green. The paper informed members of the local news and gossip and sometimes poked good fun at different members of the church. Cliff Hawker fondly remembers the baseball games in the summer and travelling to "Little Switzerland" in the winter. This was a natural ice rink on Markham Road, just north of the railway tracks, where the group would have skating parties.

Throughout the Second World War the club continued. Meetings were arranged with the youth of other churches, such as Knox United and Knox Presbyterian, to play hockey or to go skating. The activities of the club became so popular that a number of people who did not necessarily qualify as "young" attended the get-togethers. Their spirits were vibrant enough to qualify them.

After World War II many young people found conditions favourable to get married and attendance at the club began to drop off. As this decline continued, the Society ceased to meet, but those who were involved have nothing but fond memories of the St. Andrew's Young People's Society.

St. Andrew's Young People at Unionville, Victoria Day, 1897.
The location was the Unionville Presbyterian Church which is now owned by the Unionville and District Veteran's Association

THE CHOIR

One of the mainstays of any modern church is its choir. The relationship between the two is so natural that many people probably assume that the choir was always part of a church. This, however, is not the case. St. Andrew's went many years before it formed a choir and its first choirs were very different from the one enjoyed today.

For years it was felt that singing in a church service was not an appropriate behaviour. The distraction of a choir would take away from the message. Over the years, however, people pushed the idea that a choir could enhance the church-going experience.

St. Andrew's first choir was started in the 1880's while Rev. Charles Tanner was minister. Previously the service of praise was led by a precentor, Mr. Robert Purdie, who used a tuning fork. Another early precentor was Alexander Muir, who should also receive mention. The position these men filled was appointed by the congregation and approved by the Kirk Session. After much debate, a choir took its place in the service.

This "place", however, was very different years ago. The pulpit was up against the wall and set higher than the choir, which was itself higher than the congregation. The singers would sit facing the minister during the service and they would turn to face the congregation when it was their time to sing an anthem.

When they stood for the anthem, the individual members of the choir would never turn in the same direction. Bob McCowan remembers, as a child in the 1920's, that the only time the choir would face the worshippers was at Christmas, Easter, Anniversary and Thanksgiving, as anthems would only be sung at these special services. Even then the director never stood out in front of the choir.

In 1889 an organ had been added to the service. The organ was placed in front of the minister so that the organist faced him throughout the service. This decision came after much debate involving the same arguments brought out against the institution of a choir, but this time there was also the concern of the cost. Fortunately the debate ended with a decision to purchase an organ, and it has been a welcome addition ever since.

One lady, remembered fondly from her years in the choir, was Myrnie Venn. Mrs. Venn came to lead the choir in 1954 and helped to direct it through some interesting changes and productions. In fact, soon after her arrival the old arrangement wherein the choir faced the minister and not the congregation was abandoned. The membership of the choir grew from eight to thirty-two in four years, showing that changes were welcome.

Mrs. Venn had had formal music training and her professionalism and enthusiasm helped bring about the renaissance of St. Andrew's choir. She sought out and encouraged the talents of many soloists and worked hard to place different singers according to their particular abilities. Most people, however, remember her hard work that became evident in two operetta productions.

Mrs. Venn was not the only one to have sacrificed time for the choir. She did get help from many people, including Freda Jeeves, an Anglican who came to help out as an organist for a year and would end up staying for many years. Mrs. Jeeves also helped out on the operettas that made the mid-fifties such an exciting time to be a part of the congregation. These productions, performed in the new Christian Education Building which was built in 1957, are a good example of the growth of the choir and how the community had come of age. In fact the productions were successful enough to allow the church to purchase an electric organ.

There were two Gilbert and Sullivan operettas produced by the choir, "HMS Pinafore" in 1958, and "The Mikado" in 1959. These were both very elaborate productions and the people involved put in long hours to make it all work. Mrs. Venn tells an interesting story about one member of the "Mikado" cast. "We were fortunate. This girl, who was Yum-Yum (Adriane Stewart), had sung in Radio City Music Hall. She had trained in New York City, married, come to Canada and now lived up on Bellamy. We heard of her because her little girl was in Girl Guides. She said that her mother sang, so the Girl Guide leader asked Adriane to come over and sing some songs. She had a little Irish harp and she sang some songs. Anyway, the word got around that there was a woman with a terrific voice and it was a lovely show."

The production also benefitted from the sets that Dick Thomson managed to borrow from the CBC. Mrs. Venn recalls that some CBC people, upon seeing the show, came to the general consensus that, "ours was a much better performance than the CBC put on."

The choir has had many other successes, including the production of a couple of records that they sold to help purchase new gowns. On one record they performed "The Crucifixion" and on the other they sang a variety of hymns and anthems. Mrs. Venn also recalls the choir providing the music for Christmas and Easter Pantomimes performed yearly by the children while a local children's author, Lyn Cook (Mrs. Lyn Waddell) read her poems. She was known around the city for her work on radio as the "Story Lady". The costumes for the performances were created through the handiwork of Mrs. Gwen Lyons. To accommodate the plays, the pulpit and organ were removed and a board was placed over the organ pit.

Lillian Reesor started to do supply organist work in 1963, while still working at another church. She can recall finishing up one church's service and speeding away to get to St. Andrew's. When she came to the church as the full-time organist in 1969, she became more involved in the choir. Running both the Junior and Youth Choirs was an extra load for her, in addition to accompanying the Senior Choir with the Choir Director, her husband, Danny, but they enjoyed it very much. Mrs. Reesor fondly remembers that the younger girls would refer to themselves as "sisters", and they would call her "Mother Superior". The group enjoyed themselves so much that when they were out to dinner one night at the Henry VIII restaurant, the girls sang out loudly at the table. They were asked to stop, but instead the girls began to sing hymns in three parts. It was a very moving moment that made Mrs. Reesor very proud of her girls.

The current Organist and Choir Director, Joanne McLennan, came to St. Andrew's in the fall of 1990, following a summer of being the supply organist. Originally Joanne played the organ while her husband, David Bergson, served as an excellent Choir Director. Under their combined leadership, the choir membership grew again to thirty-six. David and Joanne worked hard with the choir, improving the skill level of each singer and of the choir as a whole. David also sought to have a solo performed each week, in addition to the regular anthems.

In the summer of 1995 Joanne assumed the duties of Choir Director. Joanne is an extremely talented and accomplished pianist, who teaches piano in addition to her church duties. Her students regularly win local and provincial music competitions. The congregation is often treated to a glimpse of Joanne's talent whenever she steps down to the piano to play an offertory selection. A prolonged hush usually follows the last notes of each of Joanne's performances, however brief they may be.

For over 100 years, St. Andrew's choir has been more than a collection of lovely voices, and current members are proud to continue in such a fine tradition.

St. Andrew's Church Choir, about 1891

Standing - *Mary Thomson (Mrs. Harris), Mary H. Thomson (Mrs. Jas. Young), Janet Paterson (Mrs. J.R. Thomson), Maggie Bell (Mrs. Geo. Scott), Ida Carnaghan (Mrs. T.A. Paterson), T.A. Paterson, Ruth Thomson (Mrs. Clapperton), Christina Glendinning (Mrs. Arch Bell), Bella Bell*

Seated - *--- Brown (Mrs. Stewart), Harry Thomson, Mary Glendinning (Mrs. Geo. Young), Norm Thomson, Emily Thomson (1st Mrs. Frank Weir), Frank Weir, Bella Carnaghan (Mrs. W.H. Paterson), Tom Whiteside*

St. Andrew's Choir, c. 1898
Back Row L-R - *Arthur Thomson, Anna Third, Belle Thomson (Davidson), Jim Young, Jen Paterson, Jane Anne Thomson, Jim Ionson*
Middle Row L-R - *John Mark Thomson, Florence Chester, Rev. D.B. MacDonald, Mary Glendinning, Walter Green, Fanny Stobo*
Front Row L-R - *Bella Bell, Will MacDonald, Maggie Stobo (Scott), Etta Paterson*

(Note the significant turnover in membership since 1891 - all are relatively young.)

Choir, 1897, going to Unionville, a trip of 8-9 miles.
(At least 20 people on the wagon.)

Full cast of the choir production of H.M.S. Pinafore in 1958,
with Director - Dick Jolliffe; Musical Director - Myrnie Venn;
and Accompanist - Freda Jeeves.

St. Andrew's Choir production of <u>The Mikado</u>, in 1959.
Proceeds from this operetta and the 1958 production of <u>H.M.S. Pinafore</u> financed the first electric organ in St. Andrew's. Before this, a pump organ had been used.

George Clark, Adriane Stewart and Eldean Wills in the 1959 production of <u>The Mikado</u>.

Choir Party at Myrnie and Al Venn's home on Cedarbrae Boulevard.

St. Andrew's Choir, Early 1960's
Back Row L-R - *Rev. MacNeill, -----, Jim Main, Stuart Nichol, Jim McCowan, Bob Keith, Bill MacQueen, Ron Brown, -----*
Middle Row L-R - *Lillian Jackson, Mavis Twitchen, Janet F. Main, Doris McAndless, Beth Douglas, Margaret Schoales, -----, Mildred Tyrrell, Dorothy Kerr*
Front Row L-R - *Joyce Spicer, Myrnie Venn, Freda Jeeves, Marion Stephen, Kaye MacNeill*

The Christmas play in the front of the Sanctuary in the mid-1950's.
The plays were written and directed by Lyn Waddell,
who writes children's fiction under the name of <u>Lyn Cook</u>.
Angel - Nicholas Vandermey (Now Rev. Vandermey)
Mary - Wilhemena Vandermey
Joseph - unknown
Shepherds - unknown
Children of the World - unknown

THE '39 CLUB

Another club that was a part of St. Andrew's in years past was known as the '39 Club. Sometimes referred to as the Girl's Club, it derived its name, simply enough, from the fact that it started up in January of 1939. The original twenty members held eleven regular meetings that year. Excerpts from the club's minutes demonstrate that, like all of St. Andrew's associations, the '39 Club was a careful mixture of the spiritual and the practical with some fun thrown in for good measure.

Each session required one member to give the reading. Sometimes the meeting would become a work meeting at which aprons, children's dresses, quilts and numerous infants' sweaters and bonnets were made. This was a time of great shortage as the country was in a depression, and later a World War, so in the tradition that is St. Andrew's legacy, people helped their neighbours.

Many evenings the ladies would have the opportunity to listen to a wide range of fine guest speakers. One night they invited Dr. Jessie McBean, who had spent many years as a missionary to China, to speak as well as Miss McClelland, the secretary of the Young Women's Department of Toronto. That same night the women held a Chinese tea that all enjoyed so much. It would not be their last.

The rest of the '39 Club's first year involved more work meetings and teas. Highlights included a picnic with the Mission Band in July, a paper chase in September and many guest speakers, such as Mrs. Weston from Toronto. In October the club even found the time to decorate the church for Thanksgiving.

Some of the items that the club worked to purchase were new gowns for the choir. It seems that "Birdie" (Mary Muir Cameron) received some print material from Eaton's as a donation and different girls each took a piece to make something for a sale. At other times the material came from the members themselves, as illustrated by the saving up of old silk stockings to be used by a mission for rug making.

The meetings were not simply a gathering of the women as they usually tried to put a new twist on an old theme. Besides things like the Mother and Daughter banquets, they had campfire meetings and supper in the church flats. These were less expensive than the banquets, since attendance at those cost a whopping 30 cents.

The annual report for 1941 states that there were approximately ten meetings with an membership of thirteen and an average attendance of eight. Throughout 1942 the '39 Club continued to operate. Some of the highlights included a Centre Island picnic, another Mother-Daughter banquet and the creation of the "Birthday Box." This was essentially a box for donations into which you were required to insert a number of coppers according to your age on your birthday.

The club also did its little bit for the war effort by putting together Navy ditty bags. In this way packages were sent overseas to Charlie Forsythe, Dean McKean, Jack Hunter and Bob McCowan, among others. To further illustrate their patriotism the club worked to buy flags with the help of the Women's Missionary Society and the Young People's Society.

The end of the war really signalled the end of the '39 Club. With the flurry of activity that followed the war years, people found that they had many other distractions to occupy their time. Much of the work that the club did was meant to alleviate wartime shortages both at home and abroad. The '39 Club had served its purpose.

NINTH TORONTO BOYS' BRIGADE

In the early 1950's St. Andrew's witnessed the birth of the Ninth Toronto Boys' Brigade Company. This was an organization much like the Boy Scouts, whose roots go back to Britain and Ireland. In fact many of the men and women who were part of this organization had experienced the clubs in their native countries before coming to Canada.

At this time in Toronto and the suburbs the Boys' Brigade movement saw healthy growth in the Presbyterian, Anglican, United and Baptist churches. One must remember that many of today's "hangouts" for young boys did not exist in the mid-fifties. Even the Christian Education Building, you may recall, was not built until 1957. With the "Baby Boom" in full swing the need for some organized club for boys quickly became apparent and Rev. Conkey pressed for St. Andrew's to sponsor such a group. This call did not go unheeded, and soon men such as Dave Livingston, Jim Crawford and the club's first Captain, Gavin McEwen, were actively involved in the group.

Since the boys were from 12 to 18 years old, it was decided that a group for younger gentlemen was required as well. This resulted in the formation of the Life Boys whose membership were from 8 to 11 years of age. The early leaders of this group included men such as Bob Kay (Captain), Bill Moore, Jim Crawford, George Stockdale and Bert Cooke. Together these two groups made for some very interesting and valuable experiences for the young men of St. Andrew's community.

Each week the two groups would have their own meetings and the boys held their Bible Class Sunday morning. A piano was bought by the Boys' Brigade that was used in the Church Sanctuary for many years. Ashley McCowan donated a trophy for the Best Boy each year. This was presented at the annual Inspection and as Bill Brown and Bill Moore recall, "It was more treasured than the Stanley Cup." Over the years the cup was inscribed with names such as Doug Venn, John Wright, Herb O'Hara, Doug Henry and Andrew Phillips, to name a few.

The gentlemen who participated in these groups certainly were eager. The team report of 1961 notes that it maintained a membership of 52 boys, with the majority attending St. Andrew's Sunday School. Others attended United and Anglican churches. At the Team Display 180 spectators and boys were present and eight boys were transferred to the Boys' Brigade Company. The keenness of the boys was illustrated by attendance prize awards: one boy was recognized for three years perfect attendance; six boys for two years perfect attendance and eight boys for one year perfect attendance.

The boys participated in many activities over the years, but among the most memorable were the times spent at camp in Gravenhurst. Here the Boys' Brigade Association had its own permanent camp where the boys learned outdoor skills, orienteering, swimming, survival skills and generally enjoyed the healthy outdoors. The activities were made much easier with the help of many parent volunteers such as Jim Fowles on canoeing, Howard Kerr with baseball and Alex Fernie in the kitchen. May Moore was often known as the "Maitre D," but since one "Parents Day" required May and the staff to prepare a roast beef dinner for over 110 people, "magician" would have been another suitable title.

The times spent at Gravenhurst witnessed many accomplishments by the young men. Many a future fisherman caught his first fish here and some encountered a canoe for the first time. For some of the older boys, there was the opportunity to go on a four-day portage through Algonquin Park. Here they could complete portions of their "Duke of Edinburgh" awards that were given out to boys of special distinction. In fact David Ward and Ian Thomson both obtained the highest award, the "Duke of Edinburgh Gold" award. These individual rewards were important, but the association's focus was always to encourage the boys to work as a team. The different members were all blessed with their own particular gifts, and the push was always to fulfill one's potential, but also to realize that not all had the same strengths.

In the winter the boys would travel to Camp Iawah near Westport, north of Kingston. It seemed like every March they would head up, fully packed with skates, toboggans, fishing and hockey gear and head right smack into the middle of a snowstorm. When they got there ice fishing was one of the novelties the boys enjoyed. With Wayne Tkachuk and Jim Fowles leading the way an ice block shelter would be built, sometimes only to learn that the water was too shallow. Good times were had by all as the boys would also "sail" on the ice using sheets and skates, play broomball and even make ice sculptures.

Another important factor in the training of the boys involved Drill. This helped to create a sense of self-discipline that the young men needed. St. Andrew's boys were good at it too, as, with the help of men like Gordon Telford, the boys became Toronto and District Champions many times.

Gymnastics was another popular recreation for the boys and, with the help of Alan Boyd, a member of Westminster Church, they were able to enjoy it and learn. One of the exercises that the boys did was known as "Vaulting" or "Box Work". Stan Maxwell and some senior boys built the club's first "Vaulting Horse" and the Women's Association donated the mats. Over the years, the Women's Association has always been very receptive to the needs of the Boys' Brigade. The boys were also able to purchase a second vaulting horse and springboard and they were given many mats from the YMCA, courtesy of Bill MacQueen, who was a former Boys' Brigade boy in Scotland.

The organization also incorporated badge programs to recognize skill mastery. Some of these have included physical education, scripture, band, first aid, orienteering, camping, fireman and so on. One thing they did not have a badge for was floor hockey although the boys always enjoyed it. Given that the games sometimes resulted in a quick dash to the hardware store to repair a pane of glass, maybe there should have been a carpentry badge to work on.

The idea of the boys having their own band was one that dated back to Gavin McEwen, but it took many years until the money for the instruments could be raised. In time, they were lucky enough to get the opportunity to "rescue" some from a bankrupt Lions Club. Once these were cleaned up and repaired the boys were in business.

At this time the congregation demonstrated a willingness to come forward and help out that has become its trademark. From George Williams the boys received their first flags, and with help from the Cox family, drums were acquired. "Strong and quiet," Dick Thomson said, "Don't fall short, just let me know," while Mrs. Hope presented beautiful "Colours" in memory of her late husband who had been in the Boys' Brigade. The band also received a Canadian Maple Leaf from Senator Stanbury at a ceremony in Thomson Park and Reeve Albert Campbell gave the first Scarborough flag, which was a model in his office. Finally, a former member sent a British Columbia flag and the town of Port Perry donated a Port Perry Centennial flag.

For those who participated in the band, the memories are many. Over the years, they appeared in Scarborough, Uxbridge, Bancroft, Mississauga, Whitby and especially Port Perry, where for many years they were the lead band for events like the Port Perry Santa Claus parade. Alongside this dedicated band of young men, a smart and attractive Colour Guard could usually be found. Led by Melissa Thomson, the girls included Pam, Sue and Leslie Moore, Linda McAndless, Debbie Quinton, Lynda Fowles, Charlene and Denise Reesor, Diane and Barbara Cox, Susan Landon, Dianne Keith and Kelly Anne Thomson. May Moore helped greatly with her lovely uniforms that she made to outfit the girls.

The Boys' clubs continue to the present day with many of the same activities that proved to be popular throughout the years. With the changing times, Brigade has also become more inclusive, inviting girls into their membership and assuming the name of Brigade Canada. Under the capable leadership of Lillian Reesor, the current group of young men are carrying on the fine tradition of the Boys' Brigade. Their numbers may be smaller nowadays, but their enthusiasm is just as fervent as in the old days.

St. Andrew's World War II Knitters - "Good Neighbours Club"
L-R - Mrs. Amy (Edward) Oldham, Mrs. Alice (Arthur) Thomson, Ruth Oldham holding baby (Helen Hawthorne), Mrs. Margaret Oldham, Mrs. Betty Hawthorne

St. Andrew's Boys' Brigade Band
Fall Enrollment Service Parade - early 1970's

THE COUPLES' CLUB

Another group that was popular for a number of years was the Couples' Club. This was formed in 1963 with the help of Jim and Janet Main, to create a closer fellowship among the married couples of the church. In actuality any young adult could join, but things were geared towards couples. The meetings were held from September to June, but there were not many "meetings", for it was mostly a social club. The report for the club's inaugural year says that forty-five couples attended at least one function and, on average, twenty-two couples attended. Activities included going tobogganing, playing cards, bowling, swimming, a Hallowe'en party, variety shows and seeing musicals put on by the IBM Country Club Glee Club.

No one could ever accuse the members of this association of not being inventive. One of the more interesting things that the members would do was called a progressive dinner. The different couples moved from house to house for each course in a full and diverse meal. By the end of the evening about six houses would have been visited. In time the dinners became so popular that the club had to be split into two groups. With the new housing subdivisions that sprang up around the church at this time, it is easy to explain how such an evening would be possible.

Richard S. Thomson (Dick) would entertain everyone by taking the members on world tours with the use of a slide projector and entertaining commentary. In this manner, the club was able to experience such places as Peru, the Antarctic, and Greece. The night that Greece was explored, the club was entertained by a group of Greek Folk Dancers. Sometimes the club would embark on an imaginary cruise with the members dressed in costumes befitting their station, from ordinary seaman to Captain. Since many members had only been as far as Toronto Island by boat, this diversion was certainly exciting.

In stark contrast to some of the activities enjoyed by earlier Presbyterians were the "Whistling Tummies". During one of the club's Variety Nights, Bob Keith, Bob Gray, and Bill McCowan performed this bizarre act in which they appeared shirtless, sporting giant cardboard top hats that covered their heads and shoulders. Below the hat a face was painted on each stomach with giant eyes, a nose and a mouth that circled the belly-button and appeared to be whistling. Around the waist was a frame which held a small size black jacket and a bow tie to ensure realism. The three men proceeded to dance to the tune of "Colonel Bogie" as their tummies appeared to be whistling. Once the initial shock of seeing this aberration was over, the audience found their act hilarious.

The club continued for over twenty years, but it came to an end in 1983. The name had been changed to the "Adult Fellowship Club" in 1980 in an effort to attract non-couples, but it did not have the desired effect. People had been moving farther from the old neighbourhood and were finding less time to plan these intricate evenings.

Towards the end the activities became more passive, as going out to dinner replaced "Western Night" - an acknowledgment that life had changed for many of the people involved with St. Andrew's. Still the history of the club demonstrates how very close the members of St. Andrew's have been and how bizarre their sense of humour sometimes was.

"The Whistling Tummies", *Bob Gray and Bob Keith, with artists Nancy McCowan and Eleanor Keith. The third "Tummy" was Bill McCowan. Picture was taken in the mid-1970's at a Couples' Club Meeting.*

***"Western Night"**, Couples' Club - 1970's*
Square Dance Caller - Leonard Waltham from Pickering

A skit for Couples' Club - A View of St. Andrew's property as seen from the air by "Jonathan Livingston Seagull".

THE BELL CHOIRS - 1992

The history of the choir at St. Andrew's is indeed a proud one and, in 1992, another group emerged that hopes to have a long history of service to the church. On November 29 of that year, the congregation witnessed the first full performance of the new bell choirs. These new bell ringers promise to provide a fine complement to the existing choir.

The new choirs are very interesting. The ages of the ringers range from 13 to over 70, so almost anyone can get involved in "ringing". In fact, when the choirs started, most of the participants had no previous musical experience and they had to learn both how to read music and to ring properly. It is good to see that many of the choir members are people who are not part of the singing choir, for that involves more members in the music of the service.

There are four choirs of ringers, each practising once per week with their own particular group. The different sections are divided up into octaves, with one two-octave choir, two three-octave choirs and one four-octave choir. In addition there is a bell quartet whose four members play three and four octaves of bells at a time. The teamwork required by all of this is essential, for each bell represents its own distinct part of the whole. If one bell is missing the entire effort may suffer.

The bells themselves are very precise and therefore expensive musical instruments. The ringers must wear gloves when handling the bells because, over time, the acid of the ringer's skin would damage the bronze casting of the bell. To maintain their shine, the bells are polished lightly after each use to make sure that nothing remains on the bell which will harm the finish.

On March 6, 1994, the handbells that are used by the four choirs were dedicated in a special service. Each of the four groups then performed one or two selections for the congregation. A framed plaque was presented on which are listed the friends and members of St. Andrew's who donated money towards the purchase of the bells.

In addition to the plaque, a traditional "Silent Bell" was put on display to represent the choir. This is a bronze bell (perhaps one that was a reject of the production line) that has no clapper. It is specially engraved. The bell is one of the larger bells which, if it could ring, would play the note "G", and it rests in its own special case. The case for the Silent Bell was hand crafted by Jack Tyrrell, an elder of the church and a handbell ringer.

When the handbells first came to St. Andrew's, two choirs were directed by Joanne McLennan and two by David Bergson. Under their leadership the choirs achieved higher skill levels continuously. Their success is demonstrated by the fact that two choirs were able to attend the "Forest City Handbell Festival" in London, Ontario, in June, 1995. After only three years of ringing, a "Copper", or beginner level, and a "Tin", or intermediate level choir took part in three days of rehearsal, workshops, mini concerts and the final performance with over 500 other ringers. Joanne took over the leadership of the largest four-octave choir and David Keith, one of the ringers in two choirs and the quartet, assumed the leadership of the fourth choir.

This is the beginning of a new chapter in the life of St. Andrew's. The many people that have participated in its clubs and associations have left the current congregation with a strong legacy. With the advent of things like the new bell choirs, it is apparent that today's men and women of St. Andrew's will not let that legacy falter.

A WEDDING AT ST. ANDREW'S, 1956

Some of the happiest occasions in which churches are involved are weddings. Throughout the history of St. Andrew's, there have been many such happy celebrations. With such beautiful grounds around the church and the excellent catering that is always available, it is small wonder that so many people want to get married at St. Andrew's. In their own words, a couple who were married in 1956 tell of their experience on their wedding day.

Ted and Adrianne Easton had arrived from their native Ireland not long before their wedding day of August 18, 1956. Adrianne relates:

Ted came to Canada to start a job as a tool designer which he had interviewed for and got in Belfast, just two weeks previously. Because of lack of time, it was decided I would come to Canada at the end of July and we would get married August 18, 1956.

Ted contacted my girlfriend, Aileen Mee, who lived in Scarborough, and who was attending St. Andrew's Presbyterian Church. The Rev. Frank Conkey was minister of this church, and was a friend of Aileen's from Belfast. As I was from Belfast, I was really pleased to have plans to get married at St. Andrew's.

Since I was not coming to Canada until July, Ted, with the help of Aileen, made arrangements for the wedding. It was suggested that we hold our wedding reception in the White Sunday School building, and the Ladies' Auxiliary would take care of the catering arrangements. Ted arranged a meeting with one of the ladies of the auxiliary, Nancy McCowan, and together they made arrangements for the reception.

As it turned out, Rev. Conkey was on holiday at the time of the wedding, and the Rev. Stanley Gentle from Wexford Heights Presbyterian Church did the wedding service in St. Andrew's. We were married at 12:00 noon and had a delicious luncheon, enjoyed by 22 wedding guests, two of whom were unexpected. They were from Scotland, and were visiting my Aunt.

At the time of the wedding in 1956, the junction of Lawrence Avenue and Kennedy Road was the northeastern limit of the TTC bus service. Scarborough General Hospital, run by an order of nuns, The Sisters of the Misericorde, had just opened. Lawrence Avenue from Kennedy to the hospital was just a dirt road.

McCowan Road, Brimley Road, and Midland Avenue were just muddy side roads running north from Lawrence, with only the occasional farmhouse. Before the wedding, Ted was staying in the west end of the city and it took him at least two hours to travel by streetcar and bus to the church in order to help finalize plans. He had to walk the last part from Lawrence Avenue to the church. The sight of the church spire sticking up through the trees was the only way to know that a church was there at all. In fact, when the flowers, cake, etc. for the wedding were to be delivered, initially neither the florist nor the cake supplier could find the church. The steeple finally led them to it.

After the wedding ceremony, we went out the back of the church to sign the register in the "vestry," which was a small folding table under a large tree. Luckily, it didn't rain!

Bride and Groom, Adrianne and Ted Easton, now of Unionville.

Wedding Reception in the old Sunday School building (September 1956). This picture shows the kitchen door at upper-left corner.

EASTER EGGS - 1961 & 1962

The Women's Association has worked hard over the years in different ways to help raise much-needed funds for the church. One of these efforts involved the decorating and selling of chocolate-coated cream-filled Easter Eggs. In 1962 the annual effort included a tea, highlighted by a fashion show featuring spring hats. The eggs were a profitable project for the church and the ladies enjoyed the experience very much.

The success of the fondant eggs was due in large part to organization. The ladies only needed to get together for one or two days to complete the work, as candy flower decorations were all made in advance at several homes. They would then arrange themselves on an assembly line to get as many eggs done at a time as they could. With each one doing her bit the work bee could accomplish much in a short time.

With experience, the women learned that they could save time by making up the fondant dough ahead of time and storing it in the freezer until it was required. About a week before the bee, the ladies would then plan the assembly line they would need to finish the job.

In 1961, the Women's Association made about 200 eggs and these sold out almost immediately. Most of the eggs were made in a one-quarter pound size, but they did experiment with a few of the one-half pound size. These lovely Easter treats did come with a price, however, of forty cents for a quarter pound egg and seventy-five cents for their larger cousins. All in all it was a delicious fund-raising project for the ladies of the Women's Association.

The egg sale of 1962 was so popular that it was featured in an article in the *Toronto Star*, written by Margaret Carr who, at that time, was the cooking editor for the women's section of the paper. The article, which included the recipes for making the eggs, was quite complimentary and it seemed harmless enough. Unfortunately it was read by some chocolate manufacturers who objected to the use of paraffin wax in the chocolate coating that engulfed the eggs. They maintained that, according to the rules made out by the Health Board for them as manufacturers, they were not allowed to use paraffin. The manufacturers were adamant that a correction be printed, omitting the paraffin. They felt that the ladies of St. Andrew's should abide by the same rules.

It seems that, without paraffin, the project was unworkable. This was the agent that allowed the chocolate to harden quickly to a shiny surface on the egg. Without the wax, the eggs proved to be too difficult to make and so the enterprise had to be abandoned. Sometimes, it seems, it does not pay to advertise!

COVENANTERS' SERVICE 1974

One of the special services at St. Andrew's was the Covenanters' Service that was held on Sunday, September 8, 1974, to help mark the Centenary celebrations of the Presbyterian Church in Canada. The Covenanters were a group of Scottish people who promised to maintain Presbyterian doctrines in a time when they were considered by the Catholic monarchy to be heretical.

These were followers of John Knox who fought for their religious freedom in Scotland from 1557 until the "Glorious Revolution" of 1688 that resulted in the accession of William III. It is true that the Covenanters did gain power in this period, but it was very tenuous. In fact, in 1665 the group was declared to be seditious and attendance at their services, know as Conventicles, was punishable by death. Even communicating with a known Covenanter could result in death at the hands of one of the squads of dragoons sent by the King to rid himself of these "heretics."

This dangerous situation meant that any worshipping that the Covenanters did had to be done very secretly. To accomplish this the participants made the ceremony simple and the services were often held outside, in places where a watch could be held to prevent surprise attacks by soldiers. To recreate this event properly, therefore, St. Andrew's version of such a service took place in the flat area to the south of the church. Those members of the congregation that came to watch sat on the hill. Some even wore period costumes. All in all, about two-hundred-and-fifty people attended the service.

The order of service tried to remain as true as possible to the main features of a Conventicle. The service of worship was opened by the Clerk of Session, Mr. Wm. McAndless, who read the commandments of God. The congregation was lead in the singing of the Psalms by the Precentor, Mr. Danny Reesor. Two other Presbyterian churches that have a legacy in the area were represented by Rev. W. Whyte of Melville Church in West Hill and Mr. George Hutton of Knox Church in Agincourt. These two men were given the responsibilities of reading the Old Testament lesson and the New Testament lesson respectively.

The group of participants also included Rev. W. MacNeill, who gave the Long Prayer, and the Moderator of the Synod, Rev. I. McElwain, who led the prayer of intercession. The Senior Elder of St. Andrew's, Mr. Arnold Thomson, acted as Beadle, and placed the 125-year-old Bible on the pulpit. The meaning of the word "Beadle" is quite interesting, for it can mean a layperson who ushers to keep order during services. It can also be taken to mean one who leads a university or similar procession. Mr. Thomson's role at this service seems to have been a mixture of the two.

The duties of Covenanter preacher were carried out by Dr. James Williams, of Glenview Presbyterian Church. It is interesting to note how very serious this role was, especially for the Covenanters. They felt quite strongly that the preacher's voice was the closest thing to the living God as it proclaimed the severity of the law and the grace of the Gospel.

Additional support for the service was provided by Mr. Jack Leach, an elder from St. Andrew's, who convened the Congregational Committee which arranged and planned the service. To help explain some of the historical details of the event, Mrs. Janet McCowan was present in the narthex of the Church and she was able to add some interesting commentary about the Covenanters.

The afternoon did differ from the original service in some ways. For example, the Covenanters had no musical instruments at their celebrations, but Pipers' music was used in the re-creation. The absence of music is very understandable, for their meetings were as clandestine as possible, given the situation. The service differed from a modern one in that there was no prayer after the offering, nor praise or thanks given to any person. Only One Name had any praise, the Covenanters maintained.

The message that the re-creation sought to give was summed up clearly on the back page of the order of service. It read, "Our prayer is that, gathered here in the open, the memory of our forefathers' unshakable faith and courage will inspire us to stand firm for religious liberty, pursuit of doctrine in the Church of Christ, and love of country." By remembering how tenuous and important the right to worship was for these people, it helps the modern observer appreciate their own good fortune.

ROBBIE BURNS SUPPERS

While the growth of the community of St. Andrew's has been intertwined heavily with the growth of Scarborough, it is important not to forget that St. Andrew's began as a Scottish church. This fact is important not only for understanding the church's evolution, but also its surrounding community, both Presbyterian and otherwise. The memory of these early beginnings is kept alive in many ways by those who can trace their roots back to the Old Country. One of the more common ways of celebrating one's Scottish origin is by having a Robbie Burns Supper, named for the legendary Scottish poet who lived from 1759 to 1796.

The suppers began at St. Andrew's in 1970, more by accident than by design. Rev. Wendell MacNeill recalls that he wanted to have a celebration for the church's 155th Anniversary in November. "But we were so busy in November with other things. I opened my mouth and suggested a Burns Supper in January", said Mrs. Mary Phillips. "Since I was social convenor that year, I was told, 'Great idea. You can organize it'." That first year, three hundred church members and their friends sat down to an authentic Robbie Burns meal.

This event is no mere meal, for the traditional side dish, the Haggis, is introduced to the gathering and an address is given in its honour. From 1971 to 1985, Bill MacQueen would stand up and present the address after the Haggis was piped in. With his very thick accent and the Gaelic words, many of those born in Canada could not understand all of what was said, but they understood the proper spirit of the event.

The Bill O' Fare for the evening included haggis, tomato juice, mashed potatoes, carrots, roast beef, rolls, cole slaw, Scottish trifle, shortbread, tea, coffee and fruit punch. What a feast! For those who do not know, haggis is made by combining a sheep's heart, lights (sheep's lungs), liver, 1 cup toasted oatmeal, three-quarters of a pound of chopped suet, two onions, pepper, salt and herbs. Then one must chop, mix and pack it into a sheep's stomach and boil it for three hours. The haggis was purchased from a specialty store, eliminating a lot of work and mess. For the meal in 1974, for example, the cooks used 119 pounds of roast beef, 100 pounds of mashed potatoes, and nine haggises.

There are other people who are needed to pull the event together besides the cooks and speakers. Since the beginning, May Moore has been in charge of decorating the auditorium. Maps of Scotland, tartans, Scottish Thistle cutouts, and souvenir towels decorate the walls and stage. Every year each lady has received a favour to keep and May has spent many hours each year in preparation of these items.

The convenor for the annual dinner for the past twenty-six years has been Mary Phillips. The dinners started out as a money-making project by the Board of Managers and they have been well-received throughout the years. In fact, they are usually attended by more outsiders than members of the church. This should stand as a further example of the importance of St. Andrew's, not only in a religious context, but a cultural one as well.

Haggis outa' sight

The mashed potatoes were there. The roast beef and gravy were ready to be served. The peas and corn were out. But where was the haggis?

That's what a flustered woman was stewing about as she rummaged high and low in the kitchen of St. Andrew's Presbyterian Church, 115 St. Andrews Rd., Monday evening.

It was the annual Robert (Robbie) Burns supper. The Scottish poet's 214th birthday was being celebrated.

The head table guests had been piped to their seats in traditional fashion by a piper. Now the man was waiting to lead in the haggis-bearers. The woman continued her search. Finally the haggis was located in a cardboard box covered by towels on a shelf under a counter.

As the Burns supper was a contribution affair, the haggis, in the rush of food being brought into the kitchen, apparently just got put aside and, being covered, out of sight.

The dinner guests had sung The Queen and O Canada and were seated. They had been waiting for about two minutes.

The whine of the pipes signalled the entrance of the haggis.

And with no one the wiser, the sausage-shaped haggis, a Scottish dish made of sheep entrails, rode in to be addressed, and then eaten.

The Scarborough Mirror, January 24, 1973

MINISTERS

St. Andrew's has had a variety of different men lead the congregation as minister. From the earliest days with Rev. William Jenkins to these last few of Rev. Wendell MacNeill, the position has been held by many capable men who made their mark on the way St. Andrew's operated. Their actions were really a reflection of the times and people they represented. With this in mind, one can learn more about the evolution of St. Andrew's by learning a little bit about its ministers. First, however, we would like you to learn about the search for the perfect minister.

The following little article is a reading taken from the occasion of Wendell and Kathleen MacNeill's Twenty-fifth Wedding Anniversary celebration. We are not sure how the celebrants got their hands on it.

> *The results of a computerized study indicate that the perfect minister preaches for exactly fifteen minutes. He condemns sins but never upsets anyone. He works from 8:00 AM until midnight and is married to the janitor. He makes $70.00 per week, wears good clothes, buys good books, drives a good car, and gives $70.00 a week to the poor. He has a burning desire to work with teenagers and spends all his time with senior citizens.*

> *The perfect minister smiles all the time with a straight face because he has a sense of humour that keeps him seriously dedicated to his work. He makes 15 calls daily on church families, shut-ins and the hospitalized; he spends all his time evangelizing the unchurched and is always in his office when needed.*

> *If your minister does not measure up, simply send this letter to six other congregations that are tired of their minister, too. Then bundle up your minister and send him to the church that is at the top of the list. In one week you will receive 1,643 ministers and one of them should be perfect.*

> *Have faith in this matter - one church broke the chain and got its old minister back in less than three months!*

Records indicate that the first Presbyterian minister to visit the St. Andrew's area was probably the Rev. Robert McDowell who had been sent to Canada by the Dutch Reformed Church of the United Church of the United States in 1798.[1] Another one of his colleagues, Rev. John Beattie, came up to the same area some years later.

---

[1] David Boyle, ed., The Township of Scarboro, 1796 - 1896 (William Briggs, Toronto, 1896), p. 137.

It was not until 1818 that the residents of Scarborough received a permanent minister. This occurred when the Rev. William Jenkins, fresh from the United States, organized a congregation under the name of "The Presbyterian Church in Scarboro". On December 26, 1818, Rev. Jenkins, together with Mr. John Stirrat, an elder from Whitby, approved the congregation's first elders. These men, Andrew Thomson, Robert Johnston and James Kennedy, had been nominated by the community and their first instructions were to "...inquire into the method of communicating religious instruction to the children of the neighbourhood."[2]

In all Rev. Jenkins spent twelve years as a minister in Scarborough. About a third of his time was actually spent working with what would become the St. Andrew's community, since his services were shared with a congregation in Richmond Hill. Descriptions of Rev. Jenkins indicate that he was an eager scholar with a biting sense of humour. This trait is illustrated by an incident in which one member of the congregation was sleeping right through the Reverend's sermon. After raising his voice, the man still did not stir, so Rev. Jenkins decided a different approach was in order. Raising his voice yet again, he let out, "Well, if you will not hear the word of the Lord, perhaps ye will feel it."[3] It was at this point that the man woke up, for the minister had launched his Bible at him.

The next man to accept this charge was the Rev. Dr. James George, who started to preach to the people of St. Andrew's in 1833. It was for Dr. George that the first manse was built. Unlike his predecessor, Rev. George made St. Andrew's his strongest priority and the congregation responded in kind. Having a full-time minister worked wonders for the fledgling church as the communicant role soon blossomed from seventy names to over two-hundred-and-fifty.

There were many projects that the Rev. George initiated during his tenure at St. Andrew's. He was the founder of the first Temperance Society in Scarborough and he worked very hard for the movement to establish a public library. Education, especially the ability to read, was of particular importance for the minister. He was the one who began the first Sunday School, although it only met during the summer months at first. Rev. George also taught a Bible class to the young people of the congregation.

Rev. George stayed as minister to the people of St. Andrew's until 1853 when he was appointed Professor of Mental and Moral Philosophy and Logic in Queen's College, Kingston. In December of that year, the Rev. James Bain arrived in Scarborough to take over as the new minister.

---

[2]Boyle, p. 138.

[3]Mrs. W.H. McCowan, St. Andrew's Presbyterian Church. A History from 1818, p.8.

Mr. Bain seems to have been a rather popular man, possessing a clear intellect and a remarkable vocabulary. In all, he spent twenty years as the pastor of the congregation of St. Andrew's. In 1864, when St. John's Church, in Markham Township, was built, Rev. Bain had to split his time between the two churches for he was pastor to both. Sitting seven miles distant, Rev. Bain's new charge must have made for some very harried Sundays.

Rev. Malcolm MacGillivray replaced Rev. Bain in 1875, the latter having retired a year earlier. These were busy years for the church since under Rev. MacGillivray, the congregation grew rapidly in numbers. At one point the membership role reached a zenith of 323 names under Rev. MacGillivray.[4] Some Sundays it was so crowded, it was often difficult to find a seat. With this new need for space in mind, the first room of the old Sunday School was built and some increased attention to landscaping was carried out.

From 1882 to 1887, St. Andrew's was ministered to by Rev. Charles Tanner. After his tenure, the Rev. D.B. Macdonald became the sixth minister of St. Andrew's in 1888. It was during his charge that another congregation was operating under the banner of the Methodist church. These people withdrew from that body and were received into the family of the Presbyterian church. It became Rev. Macdonald's responsibility to minister to this new charge, referred to as the Zion Wexford Presbyterian Church. At Church Union, Zion members voted to become a United Church.

Rev. Malcolm McArthur succeeded Rev. Macdonald in 1906. He made his mark by his enthusiasm for the different Women's Associations at St. Andrew's and his organization of a young men's Bible class. His tenure was another short one, lasting only until 1911.

The years 1912 to 1919 witnessed the ministry of Rev. Harvey Carmichael. Again, not much is written about these years, but we get an insight into his character from the following words on a plaque in Pickering Presbyterian Church, where he ministered in the early 1930's.

Rev. Dr. Harvey Carmichael

1869 - 1943

Born in Spencerville, Ont., graduated from Queen's University.
He came to St. Andrew's, Pickering Village in 1932. He was a quiet, studious man of wide knowledge and sound judgement. He was kind and sympathetic in his pastoral work and beloved of his people.

---

[4]Boyle, p. 143.

The one thing we do know about Dr. Carmichael's successor is that he did not work out. The *History of St. Andrew's from 1918* simply states, "Rev. W.J. Hamilton remained in the church only for one year as there seemed to be some friction among the congregation."[5]

By 1922 the situation required a strong personality. For the people of St. Andrew's, this came in the form of Rev. A.L. Burch, who had been a Major in the First World War. Dennis Phillips, whose parents, Arthur and Lucy, had been caretakers at St. Andrew's during some of the Burch years, recalled: "The family were wonderful people." Mrs. Burch taught many of the boys at Sunday School and many people remember her enthusiasm and dedication. The Burches had four children, Edgar, Constance, Frank, and Betty, and they were all involved in the church to one extent or another. Jack McCowan remembers the good times that Frank brought to many events, from Bible studies to sports and camping. The Burches, it seems, came along at the right time.

Dr. Burch died in 1939 and for a time during the Second World War, St. Andrew's was in a "state of supply" for the pulpit. Dr. J.W. Stephenson worked at the church from 1940 to 1946. He is said to have been a very kind and conscientious man. By 1947, a full-time successor, in the person of Rev. A.D. MacLellan, was found. He stayed until 1952.

Calvin Chambers was a student minister who followed Rev. MacLellan. He and his wife Alice did not live in the area and so they commuted to the church every Sunday from downtown Toronto. Mr. Chambers was fortunate to receive help from Giollo Kelly, a church deaconess. While at St. Andrew's, Mr. Chambers graduated and was appointed to the Thornhill church by the Mission Board.

In 1953, the people of St. Andrew's were very fortunate to receive a new minister into the fold, Rev. Frank Conkey. The 1950's were a very exciting time to be involved with the church and both Rev. Conkey and his wife, Agnes, were an important part of that. With such growth in the population of Scarborough, the congregation came to the decision to build the Christian Education Building. Not enough can be said about the size of this task and the Conkeys were a part of it every step of the way.

This was indeed a real time of growth for the St. Andrew's community and Rev. Conkey was up to the challenge. Many days he would spend knocking on doors in the new subdivisions to welcome the new arrivals. This dedication earned him much respect and love from the people of St. Andrew's, as well as lifetime friendships. For their part, the Conkeys had nothing but good things to say about their time in Scarborough. In particular, Agnes appreciated the way in which the community had been supportive of their daughter, Sheila, who was born with Down's Syndrome. As Rev. Conkey said of the people

---

[5]McCowan, p. 10.

of St. Andrew's, "They are not aware of what they have got or what they have achieved. It just comes as second nature."

The Reverend W. Wendell MacNeill was the longest serving minister in St. Andrew's history. He arrived on February 21, 1961 and had completed over thirty-five years of service when he retired on March 1, 1996.

Born in Westville, Nova Scotia, Wendell received his early education in that province, including a Bachelor of Arts Degree from Acadia University. As Chaplain with the Armed Forces, he served as the Officiating Clergyman at Canadian Forces Base, Toronto, for over thirty years.

He married Kathleen Clark in 1953. They had a family of three active boys, Paul, Ian, and Bruce. When they arrived in Scarborough, moving into the large, drafty and badly deteriorating manse, they were assured that a new manse was a probability. A daughter, Kimberley, was born to them but sadly, she died while still a child. Their daughter, Seonaid, joined the family in 1964. In the spring of 1967, the family was able to move into the new manse. Wendell MacNeill came to an active, thriving ministry. There was a large Sunday School, resulting from the "baby boom" years. Communicant membership increased and the church finances were sound throughout, enabling loans obtained for building the Christian Education Building and the new manse to be paid off ahead of schedule. In more recent years the General Assembly allocation was always met and special campaigns directed toward various restoration projects for the historic buildings met their objectives.

The congregation organized a Retirement Dinner which was held on November 11, 1995. Over two-hundred-and-fifty family members and friends joined together in wishing Kathleen and Wendell many years of good health and happiness in their retirement.

After Rev. MacNeill's retirement, St. Andrew's was fortunate to have the guidance of the Rev. Dr. Stephen Farris, Professor of Preaching and Worship at Knox College, as Interim Moderator. Dr. Farris quickly established himself as a warm and supportive member of the church community. The congregation was grateful for his leadership and his fine preaching. They also appreciated the generous gift of his time for many congregational events.

On April 20, 1997 the congregation of St. Andrew's voted unanimously to extend a Call the the Rev. C. Duncan Cameron of the Charge of Chatsworth and Dornoch, Ontario. The congregation looks forward with great eagerness to many happy years with the Cameron family: Duncan, his wife Cynthia Jean (McEwen), and their three children, Kyle Alexander, Laura Elizabeth and Ian James.

Ministers of St. Andrew's Church

Rev. James Bain
1853 - 1874

Rev. James George
1833 - 1854

Rev. Malcolm
MacGillivray, D.D.
1875 - 1881

Rev. Wm. Jenkins
1818 - 1833

Rev. Chas. A. Tanner
1882 - 1887

Rev. Malcolm
McArthur
1906 - 1911

Rev. D.B. Macdonald
1888 - 1906

Ministers of St. Andrew's Church

Rev. A.L. Burch
1922 - 1939

Rev. H. Carmichael
1912 - 1919

Rev. J.W. Stephenson
1940 - 1946

Rev. A.D. MacLellan
1947 - 1952

Rev. W.W. MacNeill
1961 - 1996

Rev. Frank Conkey
1953 - 1960

Rev. W.J. Hamilton
1920 - 1921
(no photo available)

Rev. and Mrs. MacNeill (Wendell and Kathleen)
Rev. MacNeill ministered to this congregation since February 1961.

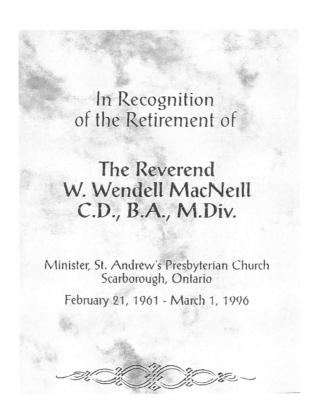

In Recognition
of the Retirement of

The Reverend
W. Wendell MacNeill
C.D., B.A., M.Div.

Minister, St. Andrew's Presbyterian Church
Scarborough, Ontario

February 21, 1961 - March 1, 1996

A FEW ST. ANDREW'S FAMILIES

It is apparent that many different families and individuals have played an important role in the development of St. Andrew's We present the next section as a sample of the types of people that have affected the church's history as it developed in the twentieth century.

The Stirling family were staunch old-school Presbyterians who were very active in the twenties and thirties. Alexander Stirling, his wife and their four children, Will, Jim, Margaret and Elizabeth, lived on a farm in an old brick house just a bit south of the Lawrence Avenue and Kennedy Road intersection. Of the four children, only Will married and not until he was up in years. He and Margaret both moved away, but Jim and Elizabeth continued to be very active in the life of St. Andrew's.

Jim and Elizabeth moved up to a farm on 14th Avenue in Markham, but they still called St. Andrew's home. For her part Elizabeth was quite a musician and she played the church organ at services for a number of years. She also spent a great deal of time with the Women's Missionary Society.

Jim was quite knowledgeable about the Scarborough families, as illustrated by a story from Nancy McCowan. "One day, after a service, Jim called me over and introduced me to a lady he described as one of my cousins. My great-grandparent's daughter, Margaret Weir, had married James Whitson and moved to Woodbridge in the mid-to-late 1800's. That particular Sunday, one of Margaret's descendants from Woodbridge was visiting St. Andrew's. She was a young woman of my age and probably a great granddaughter of James and Janet Weir, as I was also. Although I probably heard the name Whitson from my father, I had never met any of them. Jim Stirling knew more about my family than I did."

Jim was a very conservative man and, as such, he had trouble with the changing face of the church as the post-war era developed. One day, during Sunday service, there was an artist sitting near the cemetery painting a scene of the church property. Somehow, Jim found out that this man was there and he asked that the painting stop while a service was going on. The painter reported the incident to a reporter at the *Toronto Daily Star* and there was a short column written about the happening the next week.

When the newly formed Couples' Club asked if they could hold a square dance, the Session gave its permission, provided that no round dancing be done in the C.E. hall. Later on, it was decided to allow smoking in the building. Developments like these, however, did not sit well with Jim. With the building of Westminster Church he decided that St. Andrew's had strayed too far from old Presbyterian values, and so both he and

Elizabeth went to the new church. His sister, however, felt that she still had her ties at St. Andrew's, so Jim drove her to special events at St. Andrew's and then he went on to his own church.

Unquestionably, one of the families whose involvement in the church has been deep would be the McCowans. One cannot speak for long on any subject of church history without having to mention a member of the McCowan family. Frank Conkey wrote a little piece on Ashley McCowan that says a great deal about the dedication of the McCowans and what they have meant to St. Andrew's.

> Reverend Conkey recalled: *"Looking back over forty-three years of ministry, I reflect upon persons who have made a lasting impression on me. High among them is Mr. Ashley McCowan, an elder and choir member at St. Andrew's. Mr. McCowan was a quiet and gentle man, with a strong attachment to St. Andrew's church. When I went to St. Andrew's, with lots of enthusiasm and expectation, in the fifth year of my ministry, Mr. McCowan took me aside and said, 'Now don't you worry about the older people, go out to the new subdivisions and bring in new families.' It was good counsel."*

For the young minister, however, Ashley's influence sometimes extended further than simply giving advice. Rev. Conkey recalled: "When I took the initiative to have a company of the Boys' Brigade started, Mr. McCowan took me aside and said, 'Just ask (for what you need)', he said, 'but keep this between ourselves.' As it turned out, he kept his promise without having to be asked." There are many other such stories about the quiet generosity of Ashley McCowan, but since he wanted them to remain anonymous, we will not broadcast them at this point. This desire to keep things quiet, however, speaks volumes about the real meaning of charity that people like Ashley McCowan espoused.

Ashley did some things that we can talk about, however. For many years, he was the choir director. Many nights he could be found singing a duet with his wife, Florence, who was also a member of the choir. For a while Mr. McCowan was the superintendent of the Sunday School and this required a lot of time and energy. At times he could be found advising a teacher, or playing ball with some of the students. Even when he relinquished the job Ashley assisted the new superintendent, Giollo Kelly, as much as he could. (Giollo was a Presbyterian Deaconess from Toronto who helped when Calvin Chambers, a student minister, was filling in.)

Rev. Conkey remembered Ashley as a hard-working, Christian gentleman. He reminisced: *"On our visits to the McCowan home, Ashley McCowan and I indulged our strong liking for buttermilk. Paul Heagarty, a choir member for some time before returning to Northern Ireland, remarked, 'Standing beside Ashley McCowan was like standing beside a great oak.' None could have said it better."*

The Thomson family has a history with St. Andrew's that probably predates all others. In fact it was the area's first settlers, David and Mary Thomson, who graciously provided the land for the original church. Richard Servos Thomson represented so many of the good things that his family brought to St. Andrew's over the years. The following passage is taken from parts of a eulogy that John Ward wrote for Mr. Thomson upon his passing in 1985.

Richard Servos Thomson, henceforth referred to as Dick, was born in Woodstock in 1927 to Alice and Arthur Thomson. Both of his parents were great successes in their own rights, for Arthur acquired degrees at the university level in medicine, engineering, physics and English. Alice was no slouch either, for she was the first woman to teach in the University of Toronto's physics department. The elder Thomsons were quite active in the life of St. Andrew's, as Arthur was involved with the choir while Alice worked for the Women's Missionary Society. The influence that they had on their son was great, and it has been said that from them he inherited a fertile, challenging and exploring mind.

Dick was a gifted student in his own right. Excelling in biology, mathematics and physics, he nevertheless received a degree in Law from Osgoode Hall in 1953. Over the years, his wise counsel was given quite charitably to many a friend and association. In keeping with this, he was St. Andrew's resident solicitor.

Dick was an avid traveller and he saw much of the world. In fact, it was on the way back from one of these trips that he met the lady who was to become his wife, Noelle Jackson. Despite this zeal to see the world, Dick had a very strong sense of responsibility toward his home town and his family's importance to it. To this end, Dick worked enthusiastically with the Scarborough Historical Society and the Local Architectural Conservation Advisory Committee to save historical homes from demolition. Earlier, when his own ancestral home had to be replaced, he and Noelle took it apart, board by board, nail by nail, beam by beam. Since some of it dated back to 1815, they were anxious to keep the material and therefore they used some of the wood in the construction of their new home.

This sense of tradition and the need to hold on to parts of the past were carried over into his life at St. Andrew's. It was Dick who initiated the move to re-install a bell at the church to summon Sunday worshippers. He also lobbied for a reversion to the Scots custom of carrying the Bible to the pulpit as the signal for worship to start. Dick was not a reactionary, mind you, but he understood the importance of not forgetting where you came from.

Dick was an elder at the church for twenty-five years, and this alone would mark his service as important. However, he also spent fifteen years as a Sunday School teacher, and for this he is remembered fondly. His was not an unquestioning blind faith but a practical blend of intelligence and conviction. Christian morality, he believed, is the foundation on which a just and compassionate society rests. Morality means being able to distinguish right and wrong, and having the courage to do what is right. Accordingly, Dick lived a life of the highest personal integrity, with a strong sense of stewardship, loyalty, honesty and responsibility. He strove to build these values into the character of the young people who were fortunate enough to attend his classes, thus putting into practice St. Paul's admonition to "fill your minds with those things that are true, noble, right, pure, lovely and honourable." (Phil. 4:8)

This is what Dick Thomson was all about. He was not a very complicated soul but, rather, a simple gentleman who had a good sense of responsibility. His willingness to speak of these values in younger ears was his strong point. As a result, St. Andrew's was a richer place for having his kind around.

BOAT PEOPLE

One of the things that has characterized the history of the community of St. Andrew's has been its commitment to helping people. Some of this commitment has been to people who likely would never be seen, such as the W.M.S.'s aid to orphaned girls in India. At other times, assistance took place close to home. In the early 1950's the church gave space in the manse to three different Dutch families, the Vandermeys, the Dejongs, and the Uithovens. Years later the Vandermeys sent two sons into the ministry. The people of St. Andrew's acted out their Christianity by quietly helping others.

In 1979 Canadians were confronted with the suffering of many Vietnamese refugees who were referred to in the media as the "Boat People". These people had left deplorable conditions in their homeland and crowded into various small boats, hoping to find a better life elsewhere. With the large amount of publicity generated, help groups such as "Operation Lifeline" were created. This group encouraged concerned people to sponsor refugees. After discussions with the Department of Immigration, St. Andrew's became involved.

The Vietnamese had arrived without possessions and they were desperate. The people of St. Andrew's knew that they needed to act quickly. By July 31, 1979, a group of about 30 concerned members met and decided that some action should be taken. Things

49

moved with lightning speed. Within the space of two weeks, a formal application for the sponsorship of up to eight people had been submitted and $3,150 had been raised to illustrate their seriousness. September witnessed Congregational approval of the committee's actions and by October, St. Andrew's had the Ngo family to help out.

At this point the work had only begun. The speed with which the necessary preparations were completed is a testament to those involved. In one hectic week a lovely townhouse (rented and subsidized by Canada Mortgage & Housing Corporation) was acquired and furnished, and clothing and food were gathered for the family. Special mention for these developments should be made of Cameron and Joan MacLellan, Gordon and Norean Cox, Doug and Jean Hall, Bob and Christine Ferguson, Danny and Lillian Reesor, Carroll Reynolds, Betty Woodhead, and countless others.

When it came time to meet the Ngo family, Bob Ferguson, who was born in Hong Kong, proved to be an able interpreter with his knowledge of Chinese. Glen and Joyce Davis, both experienced missionaries, graciously housed the family for a few days. The Ngo family: Tri, Thi Moi, and their children, Duc Anh (17 yrs.), Tieu Nhan (15 yrs.), Kim Yen (14 yrs.), Ngoc Mai (9 yrs.), and Duc Em (8 yrs.), were proud additions to the Canadian mosaic. They enrolled immediately in English language classes, and within a short time, both Tri and Thi Moi found temporary employment with Goodwill Industries.

For the first few months the congregation, through the Refugee Committee, paid the monthly rent, other expenses and provided an allowance for the Ngos. This assistance diminished in time as the family found better work and could be increasingly self-sufficient. The congregation also had helped with loans for airfare and, later, the purchase of a townhouse. These loans were very generous and the family was quick to repay them as a demonstration of their appreciation.

This family made their own way without further support from the congregation. At this time (1995) all three daughters are married. Tieu Nhan (Nancy) has one son who receives daycare from his grandparents. Kim Yen graduated from Wilfrid Laurier University and is a Chartered Accountant, still taking educational courses while working with a major accounting firm. Ngoc Mai lives in North York with her husband and two sons. Duc Anh (Duncan) and Duc Em are both living on their own and are employed in the automotive industry. Both parents were laid off during the recent economic recession, so they have been forced to rely on welfare.

While life is not easy, they remain thankful for the opportunities this country has given them, and in particular for the bright future that they see for their family. All of their friends at St. Andrew's congratulate this family on the progress that they have made and wish them well in their life in our community.

THOMAS GIBSON - 1924

One of the problems associated with the description of the history of St. Andrew's is that there is a noticeable lack of good material relating to the very early years of the church. There are some details, but unfortunately, there are few opinionated personal accounts. However, an obituary taken from the old *Toronto Telegram* in 1924 for Thomas Gibson offers his personal insight into the changing world of St. Andrew's.

Scarboro Junction March 20- (Special) Thomas Gibson, who was a familiar figure to the residents of Scarboro Township and East Toronto, for many years, died at his home in Scarboro Junction yesterday at the advanced age of 88. He was born in the township, and was one of the pioneer members of Old St. Andrew's Church, where he was christened by the Rev. W. Jenkins in 1836. In spite of his advanced years, he conducted a small hardware store where he lived alone for a number of years.

His final visit to Old St. Andrew's was late last year, when he went to inspect a large barn which was erected over 75 years ago, and found it in perfect condition. (Note: This was probably the minister's driving shed. The sketch by Arthur Thomson of the church grounds states that the "stable was built around 1875." Perhaps Mr. Gibson said "in 1875.") *He never attended service there after the introduction of the organ. He once told the Telegram, in answer to a question, why he stayed away, "That those fancy organs and choirs ought not to be allowed in any church, as they were a disgrace to any form of religion. I don't like those frills and fads," he said. Continuing, he stated that he had sung, to the tuning fork of the late Alexander Muir, all the old songs and hymns, which he classed as better than the fancy modern "ragtime" ones.*

"In my younger days I kept the organ out of St. Andrew's Presbyterian Church for 21 years. The first one they bought, I barred the church door one wet night and ran away with the key. Organs and choirs made the Presbyterians feel they had no hand in the service. The organ did it all. We liked to enjoy the singing ourselves."

Mr. Gibson often delighted to speak of the early days at the old church. "We used to follow the usage of the "Auld Kirk" as in Scotland. At 10 a.m. the service began and with a short intermission, lasted till three o'clock in the afternoon. It was during the intervals, that the congregation gathered around a spring, and ate their frugal meal of bread and cheese washed down by water. The sermon preached in the afternoon, often lasted an hour and a half. In those early days the whole of the congregation walked to church, many coming a distance of ten miles."

Mr. Gibson is survived by many nephews and nieces throughout the province.

THE ANDREWS

St. Andrew's has done much for the development of Scarborough and it has certainly been an important part of the evolution of the community. The influence of the church and its members, however, does not stop there. For many years St. Andrew's has been encouraging the spread of Christian values and charity throughout the world. In fact a letter received during the writing of this book brought to mind the depth of this legacy. Marjorie Parsons reminisced about a service that was held at St. Andrew's when her sister, Mildred Weir, was leaving to go as a Presbyterian Missionary to serve in a Formosa hospital in 1935.

With this rich history in mind, it was interesting to read an article that appeared in the July/August 1994 edition of the *Presbyterian Record*. In it, Bob Phillips, an elder, retired from the session of St. Andrew's Church, Saskatoon, writes about the experiences of Shih Ti-San, who was helped by the Presbyterian mission.

Shih Ti-San, later called Stephen, was born in China in 1933, just as Japan was beginning to invade the countryside. As a young boy, Stephen was kidnapped by bandits who thought that his mother had some money. Although he eventually escaped, the torture that he endured had a strong effect on him and it helped fuel his determination to build a better life.

This opportunity presented itself later when he met the missionaries, Eldon and Caroline Andrews, at a local Christian school. Eventually the Andrews helped Stephen to transfer to the Tien Nan Middle School, where they taught English. Here his story was later told to Rev. Jim Munro, secretary of the Mission Department for the Presbyterian Church in Canada, and Laura Pelton, secretary of the W.M.S. They arranged for the W.M.S. to give him aid which made life a little easier.

In 1947 the Communists arrived in the area and by 1948 the Andrews returned to Canada. Stephen made his way to Hong Kong where the young 17-year-old eked out a poor existence by taking odd jobs and getting some support from the W.M.S. Knowing that he could make a good life for himself under better conditions, Stephen accepted help from the Presbyterian Church in leaving China altogether. In 1952 he arrived in Canada.

Since his arrival Stephen's life has been a good example of how many immigrants wind up enriching us all. Stephen realized his English was not terribly good, so he went to school to improve his grasp of the language.

He took more courses, wound up with a teaching certificate and became a productive member of the community. Later, he married, had two daughters and became an elder of St. Andrew's Presbyterian Church in Saskatoon.

In his own words, Stephen Shih recalls the Andrews. *"The day I met them was a turning point in my life. Prior to that, I was an orphan, starved and abused, both physically and mentally. While I obtained a scholarship to cover most of my school fees, nothing was left for food and clothing. Schoolmates made insulting remarks about me in the dormitory and in the dining room for not paying my share of the costs. For a youngster, this was devastating. The Andrews paid all these from their own pockets for many months. After I met Jim Munro and Laura Pelton, who visited our school in 1948, the W.M.S. came to my aid. The story often reminds me of the story of the Good Samaritan.*

One day, it snowed. This was unusual for that part of China. Everyone was warmly dressed and welcomed the excitement of the snow, except me. I was cold and shabbily dressed. Eldon Andrews sent me to deliver a note to Caroline at the teacherage. I learned the note asked for some warm clothes for me. I still remember how surprised the others were, and how proud I was! The Andrews also helped a number of other poor students."

The Andrews view of Christianity was two-sided: to preach the gospel and to help others. After teaching in China and Taiwan, they returned to Canada. Eldon became a probation officer in Windsor, Ontario. They moved to Toronto in 1964 and they joined St. Andrew's. A series of strokes forced Eldon to retire. He lived for a time in Seven Oaks Home for the Aged in Scarborough. Eldon passed away in April, 1995. Caroline lives in Scarborough and has been an elder of St. Andrew's since the early 1970's.

THE SCOTTS

Things have indeed changed in Scarborough over the years, but some buildings, like St. Andrew's itself, have been allowed to remain. One other such notable exception is the old Scott house on Progress Avenue, just north of the Scarborough Town Centre. This solid fieldstone building is now a restaurant, but the integrity of the building has been maintained.

Built in 1841 the house is the only original structure that is still standing in the area, although it barely survived the building of the adjacent shopping mall. With the intervention of the T. Eaton Company, the house was saved. Seeking a way to make the house serve a function and yet preserve its character, the dwelling eventually became a prominent restaurant.

George Scott, who build the house, emigrated from Dornach Parish in Dumfriesshire, Southwest Scotland. Scott was a farming man and he found that Upper Canada was much calmer than back home. His happiness can be seen by his willingness to build such a grand home and to put down his roots in Scarborough.

In a newspaper clipping Mrs. Janet McCowan recalled the Scotts from her childhood in Scarborough. She remembered two of Scott's grandchildren, Margaret Scott and Uncle John Scott. Margaret belonged to the Women's Institute and was president of the Agincourt Branch just after World War I. One of Mrs. McCowan's old photos, taken in 1910 of "St. Andrew's Old Girls", showed Maggie Scott with her sister Agnes and Mrs. Geordie Scott. Another photo from 1910 shows about forty members of the church who were children when the building was put up in 1849. Among the assembled is a bearded man in the back row by the name of John Scott, son of the patriarch and uncle to the spinster sisters.

The house itself was deep in the woods and the trees that lay just north of Ellesmere that were preserved when the mall was built were known as "Scott's Bush". In fact Mr. Scott used the plentiful woods that made up much of his property to fill his house with curly maple furniture. Mrs. McCowan also noted that the Scott house was so covered by trees that some people had never seen the house when Progress Avenue was put through.

Mrs. Jean Hunter remembered visiting the girls frequently and she recalled that it was a fine old house, "full of lovely china and silver." The girls had enough to live comfortably. They had a horse and buggy early in the century and after the First World War they drove a Ford two-seater. Company was always welcome and many remember the large, well-furnished living room which stretched from front to back of the house with two windows at either end, ideal for entertaining.

There was even a croquet lawn to the north of the house and Mrs. McCowan was one of the ladies in white dresses who played there. She remembered that the Scott girls had nice gowns and early in the century when she visited there, "the hospitality was great."

That fine tradition of hospitality continues today, except that now you have to pay for it.

JANET TAYLOR PURDIE McCOWAN

Submitted by Nancy McCowan

No history of St. Andrew's Presbyterian Church would be complete without a tribute to Mrs. Janet Purdie McCowan, sometimes known as Jenny. A true descendant of Scottish immigrants to Canada who helped pioneer Scarborough, she became interested in the history of family, Scarborough and the Church which she loved dearly.

Janet and her husband, Harold, lived on a farm bordered on the west by McCowan Road. Kingston Road cut through the middle of it. Their family of one daughter and four sons were raised to work and play hard through the week and go to church on Sunday. In the late 1940's the McCowan family began to subdivide the farm and in 1951 Janet and Harold retired to a new home, overlooking the Scarborough Bluffs on Lake Ontario.

Next to her home and family, Janet's church was most important. She knew more of St. Andrew's history than most people and also recorded much of it. History was in her blood and the Scarborough Historical Society benefitted from her knowledge and efforts. She loved to dress in old-fashioned costume and whenever there was a special historical day at the Museum or Church, you would find "Jenny" dressed in her bonnet and burgundy velvet dress, greeting the people.

Jenny was very interested in the Women's Missionary group at the church, but W.M.S. rules forbade the group to use their money locally. In the early 1950's she and a few of the W.M.S. ladies helped plan the formation of the Women's Association for the younger women so that the new group could help the church financially.

Jenny loved people, making her home available to any church or lodge (Kiwanis), Women's Institute or other group that might want to come for a meeting or party. She was "The Perfect Hostess". In the Ladies' Parlour of the C.E. Building at St. Andrew's, there is a framed poem written by a member of the Presbyterian Women, Mrs. Dorothy Brown. The poem was hand-printed in calligraphy by Mrs. Daphne Kaye, who also decorated her artwork with beautiful sprays of painted flowers. The poem was lovingly written shortly before Janet McCowan died and was meant to show the respect that the ladies had for her.

Dear Mrs. McCowan, we do want to say,
How much we have enjoyed many a day
In your beautiful home and garden fair,
As St. Andrew's women have luncheoned
    there.

In June when we came with our many dishes,
Joined by Melville friends and their good
    wishes,
A gracious hostess welcomed with delight
Assisted by Marion who put all things right.

The beauty-bush welcomed with its blossoms
    superb,
The silver birch whispered, although never
    heard;
Mother duck with her ducklings peeked from
    under the hedge,
And we all wandered down to the
    Scarborough Bluffs' edge.

Lake Ontario was seen as a wide expanse,
As we gazed in amazement or perhaps a
    trance --
We've watched Bluffers Park as it has truly
    grown --

From the lighthouse point and a lawn freshly mown.

Back to the house, stopped by the wishing well,
If roses could speak they could tales tell
Of many who have enjoyed the picturesque grounds
And of one whose generosity knows no bounds.

To the Women's Institute and Historical Society
You have given much without notoriety --
In your velvet dress or crisp summer gown
You have always been the "belle" of 'Scarboro' town.

Lunch on the patio or under the basswood tree,
Or inside the house, we will all agree,
A source of inspiration we have found;
Our hostess's good wishes truly abound.

So, Mrs. McCowan, we just want to say --
We missed you this year on our luncheon day;
We thank you for your graciousness in the past --
And want you to know these memories will last.

Dorothy "Tris" Brown, 1979

REMINISCENCES OF LONG-TIME ST. ANDREW'S MEMBERS

Jack McCowan, whose memories reach back into the 1920's and 1930's, recalls, "Dr. Burch was minister at St. Andrew's when I started Sunday School." Eventually Dr. Burch came to teach several boys at the school. Jack remembers, "He made the Bible more interesting, as well as teaching us about fellowship, sports, and camping. We had Saturday get-togethers, and he was a counsellor at Glen Mohr. The class went to camp one summer for a week." Jack also recalls that Dr. Burch was a Mason. The first Sunday in June, the Masons would attend a service. This made an impression on young Jack, as he found it "...interesting to see them all parade into church in their regalia and fill the center pews."

When Jack was a young boy, they used horses to get to church and the weather could be a real challenge. "There was plenty of snow most winters, and the roads were quite often blocked. I can remember going to church by horse and cutter and sometimes in a sleigh with a team of horses. Then, when we got to church, we would tie them up in the shed along the east side of the driveway."

"Some places on the roads, after the plows went through, the banks were as high as a car," Jack says. In fact, "...the road became very icy as the sun got stronger and melted the snow that was trapped on the road." This, of course, would ice up when the sun went down. Things did not get better, for "No sanding was done, and driving was terrible at times." The spring brought no relief because "...the frost came out of the ground, there were soft spots and, as they broke up, they were very rutty. The cars were much higher off the ground, but you could lose a muffler or get stuck."

Dennis Phillips, whose parents Arthur and Lucy Phillips were caretakers at St. Andrew's from 1924 to 1930, recalled that back in those days there were no electric lawnmowers or hedge clippers, so all work on the church grounds was done by human and not horse power. One of the most difficult chores for the senior Mr. Phillips was digging graves. Dennis recalled one particular grave which became a real problem for his father because a huge rock had appeared just below the surface. "After much thought and discussion, dynamite was used to break up the rock. The uproar was almost louder and lasted longer than the blast. Some people in the congregation thought it was improper to use explosives in the cemetery."

Dennis pointed out some of the techniques used to maintain the church in days gone by. For instance, the church used to be lit by kerosene lamps that hung on long chains from the high ceiling and could be lowered for lighting, filling and cleaning - a time-consuming job. To clean up cobwebs left by spiders, the Phillips used a long pole with a ball of cloth on the top. He also mentioned that the cellar was only a hole back then, just deep enough to allow a furnace. The furnace used wood, and sometimes coal. It heated the church through a large grill in one aisle that allowed hot air to rise up through the sanctuary. The other aisle had a grill that allowed for the return air.

The Phillips were fortunate enough to be one of the first families in the area to have a radio. Dennis remembered listening to the hockey games with neighbours Charlie Forsythe and Roy Cook. An aerial was required, and Dennis remembered that, "Dad strung up a piece of wire from the house to a tree across the road by the chicken house. However, it crossed above the telephone wire by about two feet. One day Mother turned on the radio and was surprised to hear the voice of a neighbour, Mrs. Allan Thomson. Dad had to move the aerial."

Mr. Phillips also told an interesting story of a close call that Rev. Burch had one night. Spring floods were a regular occurrence. The small stream overflowed its banks too often. Rev. Burch was returning home one evening in his new car. "He travelled east on Ellesmere Road between Midland Avenue and Brimley Road, where the stream went under a bridge. On dark nights, a buggy driver could doze off and the horse knew its way home. However, a car driver needed to remain alert. Car lights were only a little better than candle lights back then. Car brakes were used on rear wheels only. However, they were good enough this time to stop the car just as the front wheels dropped over the edge. It seems that the bridge had been washed away. God was his co-pilot that night."

Another member of the St. Andrew's community with a long association is Mary Muir Cameron. In fact, her grandparents, her parents, herself and her daughter were all married in the church, so the association is indeed a deep one. Over the years, she has been the president of the W.M.S., as well as the '39 Club.

Mary heard stories that, in the early days, people would not wear their shoes to church. Instead, they would go barefoot and wash their feet in a little stream just east of the church. These were farming men and women, and they would only own one pair of dressy shoes, so they certainly did not want to muck them up on the way to service.

The importance of St. Andrew's in the 1920's was largely social. This is not to downplay the spiritual aspects, but for a farming community the church was the social scene. To this end Mary remembers fondly the wonderful picnics and quilting bees that made up much of her time over the years. "That kind of closeness...just isn't as common. Things have changed."

Things have indeed changed, but it is interesting to note that even though church attendance may fall, it eventually comes back again. One of the most interesting things that Mrs. Cameron said during her interview was that she remembers sitting at the back of the church as a little girl. Despite being at the back, she could see all the way to the front pews because the church population had dipped dramatically. This was, in part, due to the changes in the community, such as rapid land turnover, with many old families leaving and the Church Union of 1925. The growth of St. Andrew's has not been a straight forward line, as on a graph, but rather a sometimes bumpy ride with many ups and downs.

Betty Hawthorne's association with the church dates back officially to 1934, but she was attending service there as far back as 1926. One of the things that stands out in her memory is the importance of the quilting bees that she took part in faithfully. These were held at least once a month. The women would piece the quilts from old socks and dresses. Each church had to fill its own quota of work, called a bale, whose size depended on the size of the congregation. The quilts from all of the churches would go to the city to be shipped to the needy out west.

Recently another important quilting project was conducted by the church. In the spring of 1993, the idea for a Commemorative Heritage Quilt, celebrating the church's 175th Anniversary, was put forward by one of the members, Heather Keith. The call went out for anyone who would like to take part and put together a block depicting some aspect of the church's life and history. Many hands got to work and a total of 40 regular-sized blocks and one double block were produced. Subjects varied from buildings, to cemetery stones, to sacraments, and to the choir. The blocks were joined by strips of Presbyterian Blue fabric.

In the fall of 1993, the quilt top was completed and the project quilting bee began with many ladies taking part. Several weeks elapsed before they decided to try to keep track of the hours that were involved. The actual quilting and the binding of the quilt alone took close to two hundred person hours. When you take into account that each block took up possibly ten hours of work, the total hours represented by this work of art is astounding. The quilt hangs today in the Christian Education Building.

Clifford Hawker, the son of another former caretaker of the cemetery, recalled that in 1930, his father answered an ad for the job at St. Andrew's, and Horace Thomson hired him. Given the time period, it was not an easy job, but the Hawkers made the best of the situation. For one thing they obviously could not have a well too close to the cemetery, so they had to haul water up from the spring by the library, a distance of about 200 paces.

Cliff states that his father received $8 to dig a grave in the summer and $12 in the winter, when the work was really difficult. Mr. Hawker did not mind so much for, as he told his son, it was not too bad. "I can't fall out of a hole." With this meager income, the senior Mr. Hawker needed something else to make ends meet, so he dug the graves at night and worked for the Department of Highways during the day. One night, Cliff remembers, "Someone, maybe one of the Davidson boys, who had been playing tennis in the old courts, came and stood at the edge of a grave that my father was digging out. Well, Dad looked around and, with the moonlight and all, what he saw was a white figure leaning over him as he stood in this open grave. Needless to say, my father was not impressed." As for Cliff himself, the graveyard was "No Scare": the boys often played hide and seek among the tombstones.

In those days there was, of course, no hydro, no running water and no sewer system. There was an outhouse, but it was in a shed which was across the road and about thirty yards east of the house. The well that they used was near the Library, where the "Down Lane" now meets St. Andrews Road. Clifford said that their water tasted good and that the manse's tasted terrible. However, when his father eventually had the water tested, it turned out that their water was undrinkable, but the water at the manse was good. Mr. Hawker could hardly believe the results, but further testing yielded the same results. They later found out that the cause of the bad water was all the roots which were growing and rotting at the bottom of the well.

On a dark night, Cliff said, you could sit out back and watch the lights come on in Toronto, all the way to Yonge and Bloor Streets. He also remembered that it was a big deal that they had hooked up a radio to a 6 volt car battery with a wind charger. This allowed him to listen to the radio for half an hour each night. It certainly was a different world.

Things have changed technologically over the years, but one thing has stayed the same for St. Andrew's - getting good ministers. One such man was Rev. Frank Conkey who, along with his wife Agnes, worked very hard for the congregation. Many members from his time at St. Andrew's had particularly high praise for him. In fact, one of the new subdivisions that sprang up in Scarborough at the time was nicknamed "Father Conkey".

Rev. Conkey himself remembers his time at St. Andrew's fondly, but he recalls a wedding reception in which a young girl had tea spilled on her. She declined offers to take her to the hospital and the Conkeys forgot about the matter. A little while later, an insurance claim on behalf of the girl was brought against the church. On the advice of the insurance agent, a settlement was made. Rev. Conkey refuted the claim and it was later learned that she was not an invited guest, but a friend of the photographer.

When Rev. Conkey came to St. Andrew's in 1953, he was unmarried but not alone. The large manse was also home to three Dutch families over the period. One, the Vandermeys, had eight children. This made for a very busy household. It also reflected the crowding that was going on in the congregation at the time, as families in the postwar period were generating the "Baby Boom" of the 1950's. This need for space resulted in the decision to build the Christian Education (C.E.) Building.

Built in 1957, the C.E. Building really filled an urgent need in the community. Rev. Conkey stated that, since St. Andrew's was the only church for a large area and most children went to Sunday School, there was not enough room for many of them. In a short span of about five years, the number of children who required Sunday School increased from about twenty-five to over five hundred. In fact it is interesting to note that, in an attendance book for Sunday School that was found, the number of children in one particular class rose straight throughout the year from 29 to 79 regular attendees. Enrolment levelled off in later years as churches of other denominations were built.

This era produced some memorable stories as there was rapid change in the air. With all of the new houses springing up, Rev. Conkey would go out each day to meet some of the new families and to see about their interest in joining the St. Andrew's congregation. This was done before the roads were built and things were often quite messy. Frank recalls that once he went to call on the Fyfes. Mrs. Fyfe looked out the window that afternoon to find the Reverend "...reclaiming a vertical position covered with mud from head to toe."

The Conkeys were at St. Andrew's throughout this busy time, as Frank was minister there from 1953 to 1960. Being a minister is indeed an important job, and the responsibility of his wife should not go without mention. Agnes McLeod, whom Frank married in 1955, wore many different hats during her time in the community. Over the years she was a church school teacher, a secretary and leader of two different girls' groups, Explorers and Canadian Girls In Training (C.G.I.T.). Many a night Agnes served up an impromptu meal for unexpected guests Frank brought home. This attention to the congregation did not go unnoticed, however. When the Conkeys were leaving the congregation in 1960, Frank recalls, a gentleman came up to them and exclaimed, "Well, we'll miss you, but not as much as we will Mrs. Conkey."

On a more sombre note, Bill McCowan wanted to make special mention of St. Andrew's contributions to the Canadian war effort. Many St. Andrew's members did their part to help during the two global conflicts, both at home and away. Particular attention, however, should be paid to the four members who lost their lives in the two world wars. These men were Dean McKean and Gordon Davidson in World War II, and William Heron and Fred Strickland in World War I. Their sacrifices, Bill cautions, should not be forgotten over time.

Some notes prepared by long-time church member Mrs. Margaret Oldham (now deceased), written in 1958, point out that before St. Andrew's was established, local Presbyterians would meet together in barns and homes. She stated that in 1812 meetings would often be held in an old log building, referred to as the "Haunted Schoolhouse", located near Springfield Farm.

In 1849 when the second church building was built, Mrs. Oldham stated that a "time capsule" of sorts was put under the cornerstone. In it were placed some documents, silver coins and a bottle containing some of the grains raised in the surrounding community. She also wrote that, since their initial idea of using stone for the church did not work, it was decided to make their own bricks. This idea did not get too far, so the work was contracted out to a Mr. Sisley, who agreed to make them for the price of $4 per thousand bricks. They were then hauled to the site by the men of St. Andrew's, operating as a "work bee".

Among those items found in the church records is a collection of record books that pertain to many different associations and functions. The difficulty is that they are not in any particular order. They appear as orphans, with no records preceding or following them. This makes it hard to see patterns and to draw conclusions as to what was happening. Still, what there is can be of some use to the researcher.

In the middle of Mrs. Oldham's memoirs, there is an entry by J.J. Stirling that lists the number of people on the communion roles for different years. This fluctuated greatly from 287 names in March 1879 to just 202 names nine years later in 1888. Another book notes that in 1891 the role was purged of names that were no longer relevant, so the number fell even lower to 174. Mr. Stirling's notes point out that people used to require a communion token to come up to the "fenced" communion table. Fencing the table involved excluding from the invitation those who were not members in good standing. Mrs. Oldham points out that her father was involved in the introduction of the partial use of individual communion cups. It seemed that some families were not taking the sacrament for fear of contracting tuberculosis.

In days past the church had bills to pay, just as it does today. One of the ways of raising money was to rent out pews or sections of pews to particular families. There was some prestige associated with certain seating arrangements, but the process was discontinued in 1914. One must wonder today how many members have their own "unofficial" seating spaces.

A treasurer's report of 1891 indicates that the practice of using collection envelopes was quite important to the church. It is interesting to note the amounts that people donated. An average gift was about 45 cents a week, while some people were only able to give about 10 cents. Later on the most that was usually donated was about $2 and this was often donated by Jim Stirling. By 1934 the money given, at least as far as the contribution book is concerned, became anonymous. Donations ranged from 15 cents to $3, with most in the 25 cents to $1 range. The records indicate that in hard times many people gave infrequently.

One interesting story among many that Nancy McCowan received was from Lillian Reesor, a long-time member of the church. Lillian, a former organist of the church, recalled one afternoon that stood out in particular. On this day, the church had scheduled seven weddings. As the time approached for the last one, "...a call came from a hair salon at the corner of Bathurst and Bloor, to say that the bride had not yet had her hair done. I think that I played everything that I ever knew, and composed some besides."

Calvin Chambers, a student minister who ministered to the people of St. Andrew's for a few months, adds a story about the difficulties of meeting many new faces at once.

"As you know, we didn't live in the area, but came out to the church every Sunday from downtown. One of the anecdotes which stands out in our minds is related to Alice. I brought her to Scarboro, first as my fiancee, and then as my newly married bride. She was very determined to be the best minister's wife possible

and that meant remembering names, as far as she was concerned. Her first Sunday in the congregation, she worked hard at trying to remember people's names, but the following Sunday, when we came to church, she couldn't remember a one. And then she saw a lady whom she felt sure she remembered. She walked over to her and said, 'Good morning, Miss Silver.' The lady gave her a very kind 'Hello', and talked with her for a few minutes. Then Alice moved on to someone else, but a moment later, she saw someone else walk up to this lady and heard her say, 'Good morning, Miss Stirling.' Alice was mortified by her mistake and gave up trying to remember people's names by association."

The final two stories that we have chosen to include in this section just happen to be my favourites. In my opinion they say much about what the people of St. Andrew's are like and where they have come from. The first one indicates how important charity and good will are to the members of the congregation. The second deals with how the community, and St. Andrew's, have changed over the years.

Reverend Conkey and his wife Agnes were faced with the particular challenge presented by the birth of their daughter, Sheila who was born with Down's Syndrome. The Conkeys emphasized how appreciative they were of the support they received from the Congregation. Reverend Conkey tells of the day that Sheila was born and they were made aware of her handicap. On that day he visited with one of the members of the congregation, Mrs. Davidson. She said to him, "Remember these Scriptures, 'Neither hath this man sinned, nor his parents, but that the works of God might be made manifest in him'." These words meant a great deal to the new father. "It was a word from the Lord which I have never forgotten. Many years later, we visited Mrs. Davidson, then well over ninety years old. I recalled the incident and how her words had given a lift to a heavy heart. She looked at me, eyes twinkling, and said, 'Was I all that wise?'."

Daphne Kaye writes that the houses of the "St. Andrew's Gardens" subdivision were built in the summer of 1956. She recalls, "During the previous autumn, Hurricane Hazel had roared through the countryside, causing great flooding and destruction and the small cement bridge that had been on St. Andrews Road (known as "Old St. Andrew's Road" then) just to the east of the church was washed out. The following spring the bridge was replaced by a culvert at the bottom of the hill, a little farther west than the old bridge. Until that time one had to park at the top of the hill by the church and walk down to the houses that were being built at number 120 and 122.

In the first year or two many huge trees were removed. These included a row of large pines in front of the Library building, a giant elm that stood by the old bridge and a large Carolina poplar, beside the road, was struck by lightning. From the latter tree, a piece the size of a 2" x 4" was blasted up onto the church lawn.

When number 120 was first built the old manse at the top of the hill opposite was not visible in the summer, so numerous were the trees, including an old orchard where the Christian Education Building now stands. One can still see the remains of the old well that served the church in the gully on the south side of the road.

"I remember an old lady walking by, saying to me that she had come to 'view the devastation'." (The old lady was Dr. Belle Davidson, who lived at the west end of St. Andrew's Road.) This devastation was not the work of Hurricane Hazel, but rather, the new subdivision that was springing up. Mrs. Kaye understood how the lady felt, "The building of a new subdivision must have seemed like 'devastation' to people who had known and loved the countryside as it was."

The stories and memories that have been recounted in this section are just the tip of the iceberg. The history of St. Andrew's is a long and proud one, and this book has tried to capture the spirit of the people of St. Andrew's. Our intention has been to educate those not familiar with the congregation and to bring back good memories to those for whom it is familiar. In any case, the process continues, for there is much more history to come.

The sod turning ceremony of the building of Westminster Presbyterian Church, Scarborough, on land donated by Miss Isabella M. Walton.

The Walton Family belonged to St. Andrew's. Miss Isabella Walton established a Presbyterian Sunday School on her own property. In 1958 she donated to the Presbytery of East Toronto the property where the Westminster Presbyterian Church was built.

Dr. Isabella (Thomson) Davidson, and three generations of her family taken at Dr. Davidson's 95th Birthday in 1968.
Clockwise from centre front - Dr. Isabella Thomson Davidson, Nancy Gibson McGhee, Kathleen Davidson Gibson and Karyn McGhee (Fedun)
Dr. Davidson was a medical graduate from University of Toronto in 1902 and her husband, David Davidson, was a theology graduate and missionary.

Bill Cameron, Calvin Chambers, Janet Purdie McCowan and Mary Muir Cameron

Bill Walton, Eunice Hawker, George Hawker and Nancy McCowan on the porch of the Hawker home in Gravenhurst (May 1984).

Betty and Tom Hawthorne at their home in Markham on the occasion of their 50th Wedding Anniversary, 1984.

The Commemorative Heritage Quilt was made for the occasion of the 175th Anniversary of St. Andrew's Church in 1993.

SELECTED ILLUSTRATIONS
(1840 - 1996)

The Wedding of Belle Thomson and Dr. D.J. Davidson
(Picture taken in front of the old Thomson farmhouse)

Dr. Isabella (Thomson) Davidson was a member of St. Andrew's and a 1902 Medical Graduate from the University of Toronto. Her husband, Dr. D.J. Davidson (a Theology Graduate) went to India as a Missionary for the United Church of Canada. She accompanied him. The Davidson home was the stone house at the corner of St. Andrews Road and Brimley Road.

Servers for Church Dinners
Couples served together. Corner of Minister's Driving Shed is seen in background on left.

Back Row, L-R: *Florence Chester (Muir), Walter Green*
Front Row, L-R: *Belle Thomson (Davidson), James Young*

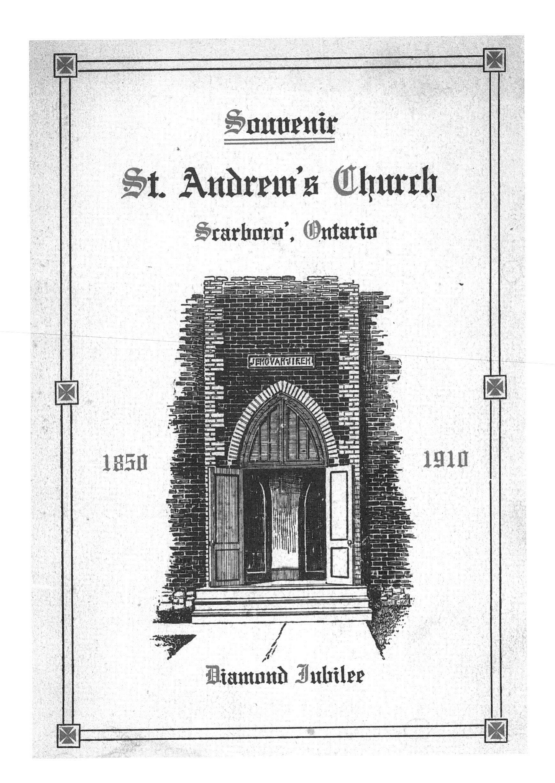

Pictures from 1910 - The Diamond Jubilee

The Children of St. Andrew's 1849 - Taken in 1910

1. John Tingle 2. Adam Bell 3. Joseph Tingle 4. Thomas Gibson 5. William Scott 6. James G. Thomson 7. John Scott 8. Thomas Davidson 9. Geordie Weir 10. John A. Paterson 11. James Carnaghan 12. John Walton 13. Leslie Armstrong 14. George Elliott 15. William Gooderham 16. Thomas Paterson 17. Robert Purdie (first baby baptised in new church) 18. Alexander Muir 19. William Green 20. Fullerton Gibson 21. Robert Miller 22. James McCowan 23. Mrs. F. (Katie Bain) Reesor 24. _____ 25. Mrs. (Mary Patton) Andew Tingle 26. Mrs. (Brownlee) Lithcow 27. Mrs. Harriet (Thomson) Ionson 28. James G. Paterson 29. John Lockie Paterson 30. Mrs. J.L. (Kennedy) Paterson 31. Mrs. Rebecca (Chester) Thomson 32. Mrs. Fullerton (Brown) Gibson 33. Mrs. Leslie (Brown) Armstrong 34. Mary Ellen Johnson 35. Mrs. William (Bella Walton) Gooderham 36. Mrs. Belle (Tingle) Mason 37. Mrs. Jacob (Mary) Brooks 38. Mrs. James (Ann) Dunning 39. Mrs. Hannah (Thomson) Pherrill 40. Mrs. John (Mary Neilson) B_____ 41. Mrs. Robert (Lizzie Stobo) Jackson 42. Mrs. George Chester 43. Beebe Carnaghan 44. Mrs. Adam (Gibson) Hood 45. Mrs. Amos Lithcow Thomson 46. Mrs. Thomas Patterson 47. (Aunty) Kirsty Thomson 48. Mrs. Henry (Mary Weir) Kennedy 49. Mrs. Geordie (Monk) Weir 50. Mrs. Robert (Brown) Martin 51. Robert Martin 52. David Martin 53. Rev. Carmichael of King 54. Rev. Malcolm MacGillivray 55. Adam Hood 56. Robert Davidson 57. James Gibson 58. Mrs. George (Russell) Scott

Young Men's Bible Class - 1910

Back Row, L-R: Frank Paterson, Alonzo Chapman, Allan Green, Arnold Thomson, Percy Weir, Mr. Cook

Third Row, L-R: Mr. Bell, Jim Weir, John Walton, Allen Thomson, Harold Hunter, Hether Thomson, Leslie Rowe

Second Row, L-R: George Scott, Richard Thomson, Tom Weir, Rev. McArthur, Dave Davidson, Mr. Wilson, Arthur Thomson

Front Row, L-R: Torrance Weir, Bert Weir, Chester Hall, Frank Butcher, Jim Stirling

St. Andrew's Session, 1910

Back Row, L-R: *John Mark Thomson, George Scott, John Walton, William Carnaghan, Peter Heron, George Young, John Green, T.A. Paterson*
Front Row, L-R: *William Green (Clerk of Session), Beebe Carnaghan, Rev. M. McArthur, William Carmichael, David Purdie*

Women's Missionary Society (1910)
(St. Andrew's Old Girls)

Back Row, L-R: Mrs. Malcolm McArthur (Minister's Wife), Ida Carnaghan, Edna Chester, Eva Weir, _____
3rd Row, L-R: Lilly Purdie, Mary Chester, Maggie Marshall, Maggie Thomson, Maggie Scott, Belle Carnaghan, Miss Murray (Minister's wife's sister), Annie Jane Paterson
2nd Row, L-R: Florence Chester, Lizzie Kirton, Belle Thomson, Harriett Thomson, Janet Paterson, Maggie Baxter, Bella Bell
Front Row, L-R: Agnes Scott, Mary Larway, Maggie Bell, Alice Carnaghan, Maggie Stobo, Maggie Bella Thomson

*St. Andrew's Choir, 1910
under the direction of T.A. Paterson of Agincourt*

Back Row, L-R: *Florence Green (McCowan), Harold McCowan, Etta Brown, John Mark Thomson, Maggie Lee*
3rd Row, L-R: *Ruth McCowan (Heron), Jim Ionson, Lexie Third, Will McCowan, Nellie Jackson, Anna Third (Thomson), Ashley McCowan*
2nd Row, L-R: *Will Scott, Jane Ann Thomson, T.A. Paterson, Rev. Malcolm McArthur, Maggie Bell (Scott), Richard Thomson, Emma Hunter (Bennett)*
Front Row, L-R: *Mable Weir (Kennedy), Clark Secor, Lizzie Kennedy, Edith Blakely*

Pageant Cast - 1919

Centre Rear: Bessie Laurie

4th Row, L-R: Ida Hall, Margaret Stirling, Jean Young, Jean Ormerod (Thomson), Isabel Young, _____, _____

3rd Row, L-R: Mabel Coathup, Queenie Ionson, Elsie Thomson, Laura Rowe (Britton), Margaret Carmichael (Oldham), Nellie Cook, _____, _____, Isabel Malcolm, _____

2nd Row, L-R: Edith Bangay, Sam Burns, Allan or Arch Cook, Alga Bangay, Mrs. Adele Carmichael, Arch or Allan Cook, _____, Mrs. Florence (Green) McCowan

Front Row, L-R: Margaret Malcolm, Ralph Carmichael, Ethel Coathup, Edith Spurgeon (Dart), Hilda Spurgeon (Dart), Iva Thomson, Marjorie Spurgeon, Bert Bangay, Mary Cook

An historical cantata pageant for the First of July, 1919, under the direction of Mrs. Harvey Carmichael, wife of the minister, and Flo McCowan, wife of Ashley McCowan

Centre Rear: Bessie Laurie
Front Row, L-R: Mabel Coathup, Ida Hall, Margaret Stirling, Queenie Ionson, Jean Young, Jean Ormerod, Isabel Young, Isabel Malcolm, Hazel Burns, _____, _____

Centennial Celebrations at St. Andrew's, 1896

David Stouffer's Choir at the Centennial Celebration at St. Andrew's Church, 1896

Sesquicentennial Celebrations at St. Andrew's, 1946

*Scarborough's Sesquicentennial Pageant
depicting the arrival of
David and Mary Thomson.
Marion Thomson (McCowan) as Mary*

Sesquicentennial - 1796 - 1946

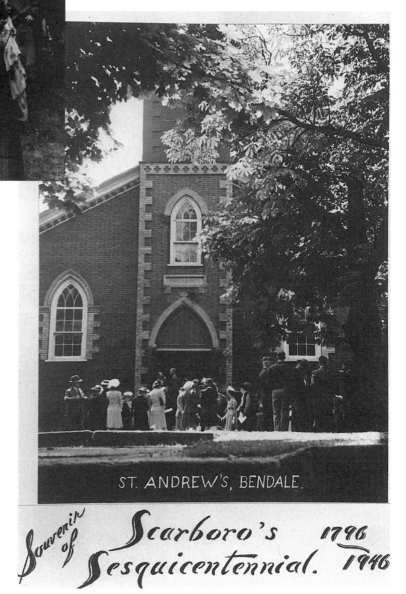

Scarborough Township Sesquicentennial Celebrations - 150th Anniversary

June 29th, 30th and July 1st, 1946
Held on the grounds of St. Andrew's Presbyterian Church, Bendale, Scarborough, Ontario

Saturday, June 29th - Cavalcade to grounds from the Township offices - opening ceremonies, address by the Hon. George S. Henry, former Premier of Ontario and member of the Legislature.

Sunday, June 30th - Sunday Divine Service at 3:00 PM on the platform in the lower grounds of St. Andrew's property. The speakers were Rev. D.J. Davidson and Rev. Norman McKay, with massed choirs of Scarborough - United, Presbyterian, Anglican and Roman Catholic churches, and Glee Clubs, twenty-three choirs in all on stage - wonderful to see and hear.
Organist - Miss Winnifred Shadlock, Choir Director - Mr. Clark Secor

Monday, July 1st - There was a Handcraft and Needlework display in the Manse, sponsored by the Ladies Organizations of Scarborough. There was also an Antique Show. The Highlight of the Celebrations was on this day. A Tableau was presented depicting:
- the coming of the Thomson family, the first white settlers to Scarborough.
- the visit of Leutenant-Governor Simcoe and family to the Highlands of Toronto - now Scarborough.
- an early meeting of settlers holding a service of the Presbyterian Church in the great outdoors.
There was a parade of local Militia and also another Tableau depicting the Life in Early Days in the Township, relating to Art, Science, Education, Literature, etc.
A Parade of all nations in national costume was the Grande Finale - very impressive indeed.

This information was supplied by Mrs. Janet (W.H.) McCowan
in her book "St. Andrew's Presbyterian Church", 1818-1972.

Scarboro Sesquicentennial Choir, 1946

Programme
of
Sesquicentennial Anniversary Celebrations
of the
TOWNSHIP OF SCARBORO
1796 - 1946

▲

MEMBERS OF COUNCIL
Reeve: Alan P. Wheler
Deputy-Reeve: Dr. Unsworth Jones

Councillors:

Ward 1:	Ward 2:
William Cowan	R. J. Sharpe
Oliver E. Crockford	Dr. U. N. Jones

▲

Clerk:	Treasurer:
Edward Knott	James O. Kessack
Engineer:	Solicitor:
Earl M. Baird, B.A.Sc.	Hollis E. Beckett

Medical Officer of Health:
Dr. C. D. Farquharson

Police Chief:	Fire Chief:
Major Charles Moss	Thomas Love

Welfare Administrator: James Gee
Assessment Commissioner: E. Knott
Building Inspector: A. Howarth

▲

SCARBORO PUBLIC UTILITIES COMMISSION
John Brown, Chairman
Commissioners:
Reeve A. P. Wheler   Arthur Leslie
Manager:
Ronald Harrison, B.A.Sc.

Front Cover of Sesquicentennial Programme

SCARBORO TOWNSHIP
SESQUICENTENNIAL CELEBRATIONS
(150th Anniversary)

1796 - 1946

To be held in

**GROUNDS OF ST. ANDREW'S CHURCH
BENDALE, SCARBORO TOWNSHIP**

▲

Saturday . . . June 29th, 1946
Sunday . . . June 30th, 1946
Monday . . . July 1st, 1946

▲

Programme

▲

"Dedicated to the Memory of the Grand Old Pioneers of Scarboro Township—Builders of this Township who by their toil and sacrifice, laid the foundation which has endured for a century and a half and will live for evermore."

Back Cover of Sesquicentennial Programme

TOWNS[HIP]

SESQUICENTENNIAL (150TH)

17[...]

$\mathcal{D}i$[...]

ST. ANDRE[W]

Sunday, Jun[e]

Organist,

1. ANTHEM: "Holy Art Thou" ———————————— *Handel's Largo*
   Massed Choirs of Scarboro

2. CALL TO WORSHIP:
   "Remember the days of old, consider the years of many generations."
   "O give thanks unto the Lord for He is good; for His mercy endureth for ever."

3. HYMN: "All people that on earth do dwell."

All people that on earth do dwell,
   Sing to the Lord with cheerful voice.
Him serve with mirth, His praise forth tell;
   Come ye before Him and rejoice.

2 Know that the Lord is God indeed;
   Without our aid He did us make;
We are His folk, He doth us feed,
   And for His sheep He doth us take.

3 O enter then His gates with praise,
   Approach with joy His courts unto;
Praise, laud, and bless His Name always,
   For it is seemly so to do.

4 For why the Lord our God is good;
   His mercy is for ever sure;
His truth at all times firmly stood,
   And shall from age to age endure. Amen.

4. PSALM: 107: v. 1-19, v. 23-43.

5. HYMN: "O God, our help in ages past."

O God, our help in ages past,
   Our hope for years to come,
Our shelter from the stormy blast,
   And our eternal home:

2 Under the shadow of Thy throne
   Thy saints have dwelt secure;
Sufficient is Thine arm alone,
   And our defence is sure.

3 Before the hills in order stood,
   Or earth received her frame,
From everlasting Thou art God,
   To endless years the same

4 A thousand ages in Thy sight
   Are like an evening gone,
Short as the watch that ends the night
   Before the rising sun.

5 Time, like an ever-rolling stream,
   Bears all its sons away;
They fly forgotten, as a dream
   Dies at the opening day.

6 O God, our help in ages past,
   Our hope for years to come,
Be Thou our guard while troubles last,
   And our eternal home. Amen.

6. SCRIPTURE READING: Deuteronomy 8.

7. ANTHEM: "Dear Land of Home" ———————————— *Sibelius Finlandia*
   Massed Choirs of Scarboro

GO[...]

Sesquicentennial Programme

CARBORO

ANNIVERSARY CELEBRATIONS
1946

Service

CH, BENDALE

1946 at 3 p.m.

d Shadlock

8. ADDRESS: Rev. David Davidson.

9. Prayers of Remembrance, Thanksgiving and Intercession.

10. HYMN: "Now thank we all our God."

Now thank we all our God,
  With heart, and hands, and voices,
Who wonderous things hath done,
  In whom His world rejoices;
Who from our mother's arms
  Hath blessed us on our way
With countless gifts of love,
  And still is ours today.

2 O may this bounteous God
  Through all our life be near us,
With ever joyful hearts
  And blessed peace to cheer us;
And keep us in His grace,
  And guide us when perplexed,
And free us from all ills
  In this world and the next.

3 All praise and thanks to God
  The Father now be given,
The Son, and Him who reigns
  With them in highest heaven,
The one eternal God,
  Whom earth and heaven adore;
For thus it was, is now,
  And shall be evermore.   Amen.

11. SERMON: Rev. Norman MacKay, Toronto.
     (Former Overseas Padre)

12. HYMN: "From Ocean Unto Ocean."

From ocean unto ocean
  Our land shall own Thee Lord,
And, filled with true devotion,
  Obey Thy sovereign word;
Our prairies and our mountains,
  Forest and fertile field,
Our rivers, lakes, and fountains
  To Thee shall tribute yield.

2 O Christ, for Thine own glory,
  And for our country's weal,
We humbly plead before Thee,
  Thyself in us reveal;
And may we know, Lord Jesus,
  The touch of Thy dear hand,
And, healed of our diseases,
  The tempter's power withstand.

3 Where error smites with blindness,
  Enslaves and leads astray,
Do thou in loving-kindness
  Proclaim Thy gospel day,
Till all the tribes and races
  That dwell in this fair land,
Adorned with Christian graces,
  Within Thy courts shall stand.

4 Our Saviour King, defend us,
  And guide where we should go,
Forth with Thy message send us,
  Thy love and light to show,
Till, fired with true devotion
  Enkindled by Thy word,
From ocean unto ocean
  Our land shall own Thee Lord.   Amen.

A Prayer of Dedication

KING

Other Occasions

Farewell Dinner for Rev. Frank Conkey, Mrs. Agnes Conkey and Sheila, 1960. Clerk of Session James Stirling stands with them.

C.G.I.T., about 1957. Frank and Agnes Conkey with baby, Sheila.

Some of those from St. Andrew's who have gone on to further service, here and abroad, then and now

Lissa Glendenning
First Presbyterian Deaconess
April 26, 1909

Ethel Glendenning
Missionary - India
December 15, 1908

Harriet Thomson
Missionary - India
1896 - 1929

Dorothy Jenkins
Deaconess - Missionary
April 18, 1929

Mildred Weir, R.N.
Medical Missionary - Formosa
October 9, 1935

Rev. Gwen Brown
Ordained February, 1987

Rev. Catherine Chalin
Ordained September, 1992

Rev. Ruth Draffin
Ordained April, 1994

Rev. Scott McAndless
Ordained September, 1992

Rev. Karen McAndless Davis
Ordained May, 1991

Rev. Joyce Davis
Ordained February, 1996

Rev. Bruce McAndless Davis
Ordained July, 1996

1841	Account of Seat rent rec'd from Collectors				1841
June 28	Rec'd from George Scott	2	10		January
	Arch'd Malcom	2	2	6	
	John Tabor a gift by A. Malcom	1	10	½	
	W'm Demma " do		2	6	
	John Dingle	1	15		
	John Glendining	3	11	3	
	John Stobo	3	6	3	
	John Skelton	1	8	9	
	Hugh Elliot	2	15		
	John Martin	1	12	6	
	William Paterson	3			
	George Scott		7	6	
	David Brown	2	2	6	
	Alex'r Stirling	1	13	1½	
	James A. Thomson Collection money	4	14	6	
		31	3	3	
Oct 4	Arch'd Malcom	1	10		April
	Hugh Elliot	1	17	6	
	David Brown	2	2	6	
	John Glendining	2	2	6	
	John Skelton	1	15		
	John Stobo	2	13	9	
	W'm Paterson	4	1	3	
	George Scott	4	7	6	
	do do		5		
	John Glendining		2	6	
	John Martin	1	17	6	
	Alex'r Stirling	2	6	3	
		25	1	3	

Sample from the Pew Rental Log (1840)

A Winter Scene at St. Andrew's

St. Andrew's Church 1819-1849

INTRODUCTION TO PART II

All who meander along St. Andrew's Road near the Church must suspect that the clock has slipped back about a century: the narrow tree-lined gutterless road, the quaint board and batten "Sexton's House," the well-manicured "Kirkyard" with ancient monuments to pioneers, the 100 year old "Centennial Memorial Library" and, of course, St. Andrew's Church itself, now 148 years young.

But one of the more astonishing aspects of this oasis in the midst of a city is the actual *size* of the Church property. In 1819, several acres of bush and sandy soil on an isolated knoll were certainly surplus to the needs of the Scarborough pioneer, David Thomson. His sincere gift of land for a "Scotch Kirk" was very much appreciated -- particularly by those of us who so enjoy this paradise today. What hardy backwoods-person would have thought that, 178 years later, their Church would be in the center of a city of half a million? Which of the original trustees would have dreamed that their late 20th century successors would have responsibility for such valuable land?

The operation and maintenance of the St. Andrew's property is a story of fulfillment, frustration, consensus and dispute. However, it has been a story of innovation, perseverance -- and success.

Bruce McCowan

Aerial View of St. Andrew's

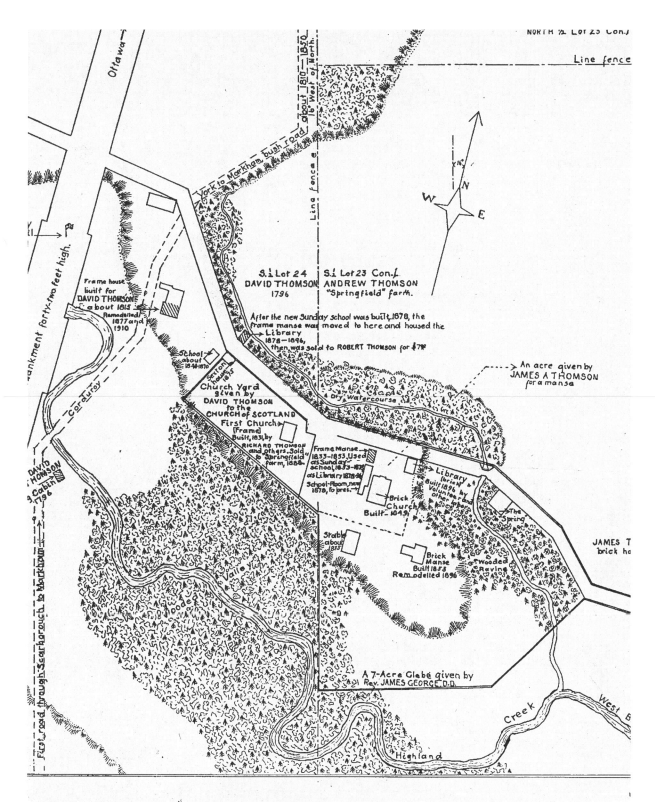

Plan of the valley and surrounding hillsides of the original Thomson Settlement in Scarboro Township.

Sketch map of St. Andrew's Site drawn by Arthur Thompson in 1946

Expenditure

			forward	1328 37
	By	Wood 6¼ cords @ 4½ Miss M. Scott		28 12
	"	~~Balance of the cost of soldiers memorials~~		~~28 97~~
Mar. 1	"	Rev. H. Carmichael Bonus		259 00
Dec. 18	"	31 gold Lockets J. D. Scott		240 97
" 20	"	Brass tablet in memory of 31 who served in war		150 00
" 23	"	Galv. pipes for Manse furnace Wheeler & Bain		10 00
" 30	"	~~David Marshall balance for soldiers Memorials~~		~~28 97~~
Feby. 7	"	Presbyterian Record 57 copies		20 00
Dec. 28	"	Rev. D. L. Gorden for his pulpit supply		11 00
	"	Sunday School Supplies for 1920		65 99
		Total Expenditure	$2113	45
		Balance on hand	$262	84
			$2376	29
	Subscription for farewell purse for Rev. H. Carmichael		115	00
			2491	29

Examined & found correct
Jan. 14/20

H. F. Scott } Auditors
Frank Weir

Taken from Treasurer's Book for the year 1919
Note the expenditure for the Brass Tablet in memory of the 31 who served in WW I; also the 31 gold lockets that were given to them.

World War I Memorial Plaque

World War II Memorial Plaque

Plaques for Two World Wars
St. Andrew's Church, Scarboro
In Honour of Those Who Served in the Great War
1914 - 1918

James Baird	Ernest Scrivens
Robert Baird	Frank Sellers
Frank Bell	Philip Short
George Bell	Arthur Smith
William Britton	Thomas C. Smith
Fred Burns	James Stirling
Stanley Chester	William Stirling
Harvey Coathup	Isaac A. Stobo
Chester Hall	* Fred Strickland
* William Heron	Arthur W. Thomson
Alexander Howitt	Hether Thomson
William L. Lawrie	Herbert J. Weir
Frank G. Paterson	John Weir
George R. Paterson	Percy G. Weir
Clarence Rowe	Annie M. Baird
	Dorothy Jenkinson

* Killed   31 Names   29 men and 2 women

St. Andrew's Church, Scarboro
In Honour of Those Who Served in World War
1939 - 1945

Vera O. Cole	John McCowan
Arthur Davidson	Robert McCowan
* Gordon Davidson	Walter McCowan
Charles Forsythe	William McCowan
Clifford Hawker	* Dean McKean
John Heron	Dennis Phillips
John Hunter	James Woolhead
Neil Hunter	

* Killed   15 Names   14 men and 1 woman

Harold McCowan's Treasurer's Book, from the "Dirty Thirties", a difficult period for many Canadians, affords us a glimpse of this story.

Maintenance & Operation: The Treasurer's Book

Extracts Selected by Nancy McCowan

1933

Some Expenses

George Hawker for Stove	$ 8.00
Hydro Electric	6.23
	6.08
	5.36
	6.23
Torrance Weir load gravel	2.50
W.D. Cowan load gravel	2.50
H. Thomson Building verandah	28.96
F. Morgan Bunch Shingles	1.15
J. Elliott & Son wood & cement	16.63
Taxes	72.22

Some Receipts

Library share of hydro for 1933	$ 7.98
Young Peoples Society donation	20.00
Library rent	1.00

There was a deficit of $250.98 in 1933.

1934

Some Expenses

Padget & Hay Supplies for verandah	$ 9.65
Frank Weir fruit trees & paint	12.00
Elliott & Son 1 ton coal, 2 bags cement	14.80
John Blake 2 tons coal	27.00
Duplex envelopes	8.50

1934 - Some Expenses

Hydro Electric	$ 7.31
	7.39
	5.87
	6.23

Some Receipts

St. Andrew's Bible Class Donation	$ 20.00
Rent & electric light from Library	9.93
Young Peoples Society Donation	40.00
Collection per Envelope	952.65
Open Collection	216.64

There was a balance of $3.66 at the end of December, 1934.

1935

Some Expenses

Robert Weir Insurance	$ 77.93
Rev. Burch Monthly stipend	100.00
Scarboro taxes	51.10
Burnett Bros. Cleaning well	6.00

Some Receipts

Christina Thomson Legacy	$ 12.60
Library rent & share of Hydro	9.30
Collection per Envelope	956.05
Open Collection	272.58

There was a balance of $3.79 at the end of December, 1935.

Auditors: A.G. Thomson, James J. Stirling

1936

Some Expenses

Geo. Hawker yearly wages	$ 75.00
W.D. Morrish provisions for Anniversary	20.70

Some Receipts
Interest on Bond	$ 7.50
Receipts from Anniversary	59.70
Sale of Shed (part)	60.00
Library share of hydro	7.35
Library rent	1.00
Collection per Envelope	860.45
Open Collection	287.28
Young Peoples Society Donation	35.00

There was a balance of $51.09 at the end of December, 1936.

1937
Some Expenses
Padget & Hay	furnace	$235.00
R.A. McCowan	pump	17.77
Padget & Hay	paint, supplies	8.50
H. Blumson	painting	225.00
Horace Thomson	repairs	80.00
Padget & Hay	eavestrough	53.53
Robert Radcliffe	wood	11.00
Frank Weir	paint, supplies	52.00

Some Receipts
5 Donations for furnace	$231.00
Library share of hydro	7.04
Library rent	1.00
Young Peoples Society Donation	20.00
Anniversary Receipts	77.40

There was a balance of $3.23 at the end of December, 1937.

Auditors: A.G. Thomson & J.B. Heron

1938
Some Expenses
F. Weir	Insurance	$ 73.83
Padget & Hay	pump	89.90
Coal		24.00

Some Receipts
Collection per Envelope	$977.21
Open Collection	254.62
Receipts from other sources	118.50
Cash in Bank, Jan. 1, 1938	3.23

There was a balance of $4.50 at the end of December, 1938.

1939
Some Expenses
Mkhm. Economist & Sun - printing		$4.75
Joe Page	painting	2.50
W. Ferguson	painting roof	35.00
C.C. Miner	painting steeple	50.00
John Elliott	sand & lime	3.55

Starting October 23, 14 payments of $12.00 to Rev. Carmichael

Some Receipts
Receipts from church supper	$ 49.61
8 donations for church steeple	45.00
Donations for flowers	8.00
Young Peoples Society Donation	10.00

There was a balance of $116.81 at the end of December, 1939.

As we can see, the cost of maintaining St. Andrew's buildings over the years has been a challenge, with overall revenues falling short of expenses at times.

Certainly, whenever a significant capital expense came along, there would be some serious discussion about the shortage of cash and the downside of being a congregation in debt.

The construction of the present church in 1849 was probably preceded by such a debate. Even seven years later, at the 1856 Annual Meeting, it was resolved that:

...subscription lists be opened forthwith for the purpose of raising money to liquidate the debt of the Church and that Messrs. William McCowan, Robert McCowan, Andrew Paterson, Josh Sisley, James McCowan, John Elliot and William Oliver be a committee to carry the above resolution into effect.

So, just what did the Congregation's gamble get in 1849?

A view of St. Andrew's in winter from the wooded area across from the church. Picture taken sometime before the demolition of the white Sunday School building.

The finely manicured grounds at the time of the Diamond Jubilee of the Congregation in 1910

THE ARCHITECTURE OF ST. ANDREW'S SANCTUARY

Submitted by George W.J. Duncan
A Member of the Canadian Association of Professional Heritage Consultants

St. Andrew's is a fine example of the picturesque Early Gothic Revival style. Its form is essentially Classical with a rectangular plan, gable-end entrance and medium-pitched gable roof, but incorporates Gothic Revival features such as pointed-arch windows, hood moulds and buttresses.

While many other rural churches in the vicinity were built in frame, the forward-looking congregation of St. Andrew's opted for a more substantial, but significantly more costly structure of solid brick. The Flemish bond brickwork, expensive in its day, was noted by respected architectural historian, the late John I. Rempel.

The colourful patterned brick treatment is a striking feature of the church. Its use on such an early building is an indication that the designer/builder may have been familiar with the latest architectural trends in Britain in the 1840's.

English architectural theorist, John Ruskin, was the main proponent of polychromy (the decorative use of multi-coloured masonry) for ecclesiastical buildings. Ruskin's inspiration was based on medieval examples in northern Europe.

In the case of St. Andrew's, the main brick colour is a warm red. For contrast, buff coloured brick was employed (called white brick in the 19th century), along with a limited use of dressed limestone for label stops, buttress copings and datestone.

The white brick accents provide three-dimensional detail through their slight projection from the main wall face. Corner quoins, buttresses, hood moulds over the main door and windows and the frieze below the eaves were all done in the contrasting lighter brick. In addition, a quoin-like treatment was used to frame the windows. This particular feature is associated with many of the mid 19th century brick homes of Scarborough's Scottish settlers.

Interestingly, the brick quoining was simulated in wood for the portion of the steeple tower above the eaves line. The stepped tower is capped with a steep, metal-clad spire which, along with its distinctive weathervane, is a landmark rising above the trees at the edge of the Highland Creek ravine.

The main entrance is contained within a shallow projecting bay that forms the base of the tower. The entrance consists of a pair of wood doors divided into panels with stout rope mouldings. The Gothic arch above the doors is infilled with a similar solid wood treatment.

Carved stone grotesques depicting male and female faces form the label stops on either side of the door, a sophisticated feature for a rural church.

Above the entrance is a paneled datestone reading "JEHOVAH JIREH" (The Lord Will Provide) and the date of construction - 1849.

There are two styles of early windows found on the church. The main windows are mullioned with a Y-shaped division. Narrow panes of coloured glass, framing the perimeter of the sash, are glazed chiefly in large sheets of textured translucent glass.

Secondary windows, visible on the front of the building, have interlacing tracery in the upper portions of the sash. Two similar windows on the rear wall have been replaced recently with stained glass memorials.

The exterior of St. Andrew's has remained little changed since 1849, but the interior has been altered to reflect changes in worship through the generations. Notable periods of change were the 1890's, when the church was remodeled, and the 1990's, when renovations and a general "sprucing up" were undertaken.

The 1990's renovations required much work to the plaster, which allowed an opportunity to view some of the early interior treatment that had been covered up by later layers. The work revealed the original plaster, applied directly to the brick, and random-width beaded wainscoting.

Today, the mellow pine floors, V-groove wainscoting and plaster arch framing the pulpit are significant interior architectural features. The pleasing 19th century architecture of St. Andrew's is enhanced by its park-like setting on a winding stretch of St. Andrew's Road. Much of the rural ambience of the area has survived the urbanization of Scarborough.

Other adjacent historic sites include the cemetery, resting place of many early settlers, the 1880's Sexton's House and the 1896 Centennial Memorial Library.

Rev. James George, D.D., Minister of St. Andrew's, 1833 - 1853

Peter Scott, the Builder of the 1849 St. Andrew's brick church. The original photograph names the builder, Peter Scott, Wife, and dog, Tiny; Mrs. Scott's name is not given. The Scotts lived with William Thomson, in the stone house, while building the church. The picture was presented to St. Andrew's by Mrs. T.A. Paterson, "Sawmill Willie's" granddaughter.

St. Andrew's and the Old Sunday School Building
In the days when a white picket fence surrounded the church buildings and an apple orchard was on the east side of the church.

The spruce trees west of the church were planted in about 1890, having been supplied by Henry Westney of West Hill, "a retired tree importer" according to a circa 1915 newspaper clipping.

The maple tree in the centre of the photo is still there. In 1994, this tree was named in the Scarborough Parks and Recreation Culture Committee's Contest, entitled "Scarborough's Tremendous Tree Hunt". It was nominated by at least three people. The tree has recently been pruned drastically for safety reasons.

BOYS WILL BE BOYS!
Submitted by Nancy McCowan

The two "carved stone grotesques" mentioned in the previous section were installed beside the door when the church was built by contractor Peter Scott. One of the Church legends holds that these two sculpted heads are those of Peter Scott himself and Charles Spence, his assistant.

However, the figure on the west does appear to be a woman. It could be that the heads represent "any man or woman" who enters the church. The nose of the figure on the west side is broken.

During a discussion with Betty Hawthorne, she recalled a conversation she had with Margaret Carmichael Oldham. Margaret came to St. Andrew's in March, 1912, with her father, Rev. Harvey Carmichael and stepmother. She was twelve years old at the time. Her half-brother, Ralph, was born later that year.

Little boys of that era had to find some way to amuse themselves and from the cost of replacing broken windows in the church through the years, it is evident that many of them put in time by casting stones, pebbles or chestnuts at the church. According to Margaret's story, her brother Ralph was the unlucky one whose stone broke the nose off the lady's face.

Ralph Carmichael followed his father in the Ministry, preaching most of his life in the United States. He died just recently, in 1995, and was buried at St. Andrew's at his request.

Two Carved Stone Grotesques which flank the front door of the church

RENOVATION AND RESTORATION - 1990

Submitted by Ruth Finn

Following two years of discussions, a restoration of the sanctuary began in March 1990. The architectural firm of Brown, Beck and Ross had been employed to draw plans and make models which had been considered (prior to this date) at congregational meetings. Some funds had been raised.

The Board of Managers decided that the church roof should be re-shingled prior to the interior work commencing. Quotes were obtained and the contract let to R&R Roofing. As work began and two layers of asphalt shingles removed, it was obvious that the rectangular pieces of tin which originally covered the roof must be removed. Plywood sheets were then applied, followed by the heaviest weight of asphalt shingles available (20 lb.) in a charcoal shade. The cost was $10,000.

Mr. Douglas B. Brown, of Brown, Beck and Ross, obtained several quotations on the interior work, including removal of the old plaster. The contract was given to Marna Construction Ltd., who submitted the lowest quote, and was highly recommended by the architect.

Under the chairmanship of Mr. A. Leach, a "Miracle Sunday" to raise remaining funds for the project was held in May, 1990. The response from the congregation proved to be a modern-day miracle as all of the funds needed were given or pledged on that Sunday.

This response was truly heart-warming and proved once again the dedication and commitment of the people of St. Andrew's. A committee consisting of Jack Marks, Joyce Marks, Ed Locke, John Hopkins, Rev. W. MacNeill and Ruth Finn was formed.

Late in May the pews were removed from the sanctuary, scaffolding was erected and work begun to remove the plaster. The arch at the front of the church and some ceiling ornamentation were removed, to be re-applied following plastering. The south exit door was moved slightly to accommodate the new platform design. When the wooden lath was exposed, frames of the two south windows were again apparent. They had been plastered over prior to 1900 following complaints by the parishioners that the sunlight was intolerable. As portions of the wainscoting were removed where necessary, it was obvious that underneath was one of the somewhat wider boards which had been painted white.

Following a summer of some stresses, much dust and dirt and an equal amount of joy in the re-creation of our church, finishing details were applied. Jack Marks' enthusiasm regarding the south windows remaining open proved infectious within the committee and memorial gifts to install stained glass windows were received.

Valley City Manufacturing Company, under directions of Mr. Brown, installed our existing pews in a manner to conform to the shape of the platform area. They also manufactured and installed the choir frontals.

New electrical fixtures were selected to conform to the Victorian period of the church and to provide greater light than the existing globes. These globes, which had been installed following the change over to electricity, are now being used in the narthex. Ceiling fans were installed as well. A new sound system, supplied by Alectro, was purchased and installed with the assistance of Mr. Jack Tyrrell.

Interfloor Carpet Contracts Inc. supplied and installed carpets in the sanctuary and in the narthex. The curved platform levels were hand stitched. Plywood was applied in the narthex to provide a more level base than the old pine boards.

A wide baseboard was specially milled to duplicate the original which was cracked and badly damaged. Wainscoting and floors in the sanctuary were varathaned. New doors were hung between the sanctuary and the narthex. The Presbyterian Women donated a new piano for the sanctuary.

As the pews had been covered with a great deal of grime and plaster dust, a scrubbing and polishing bee was held on a very warm day in late August. Renovations were almost complete by early September and services commenced some weeks later. Dedication by the Moderator, Dr. John Allan, on November 25 1990, was a joyous event, followed by a luncheon in the Christian Education Hall. It was attended by Mayor Joyce Trimmer, Mr. Brown, architect, and Mr. M. Schultz of Marna Construction.

Upholstering of the choir pews and the addition of two flower stands have since occurred. We also have hung two beautiful framed alabaster plaques in the narthex - the gift of a member of the congregation. New choir gowns were purchased to complement our new interior.

The costs of refurbishing and additional equipment came to just over $130,000.

"Miracle Sunday" and the fund-raising for the 1990 renovation appears to have been more successful than the fund-raising for the previous major renovation -- 97 years earlier -- when, in February 1894:

> *The Treasurer reported about the way the finances were coming in showing a deficiency in receipts. It was agreed to have the Pastor give the congregation a hint from the pulpit to try and increase the subscriptions or to have them come in more regular.*

The pews presently in the Church date from the 1893 renovation. It was probably at that time that the two windows at the front were plastered over.

The removal of old plaster during the church restoration project - 1990.

The contractors having completed the plastering and painting of the Sanctuary, Verna Barrette and Ruth Finn are seen cleaning the pews.

The last service (April 15, 1990) in St. Andrew's prior to restoration work.

October 21, 1990 - The first service in the restored sanctuary

Ruth Finn and Mayor Frank Faubert with descendants of Scarborough pioneers, Bill McCowan, Bob McCowan, Nancy Weir McCowan, Noelle Thomson (wife of the late Richard S. Thomson). The City of Scarborough presented St. Andrew's with a Heritage Conservation Award in February, 1995, in recognition of the Sanctuary Restoration.

MEMORIAL STAINED GLASS WINDOWS

Submitted by Mrs. Jean Oldham Nauta

At the close of the "Miracle Sunday" service, Jack Marks approached descendants of three early families with a very interesting suggestion. Two Gothic windows on the south wall (directly behind the communion table) had been boarded up many years earlier to prevent the glare which fell over the congregation. If they were to be opened up once again, would these families be interested in installing stained glass memorial windows to be dedicated to their loved ones who had so faithfully served this church in their place? The answer was a definite "YES" from the Richard S. Thomson family, from the Harold and Jenny McCowan family and from the family of Ewart and Margaret Oldham.

The committee formed to make a study of what was available and to come to a final choice of windows was made up of Noelle Thomson, Bob McCowan, Edward Oldham, and Jean (Oldham) Nauta.

The designer of the most elegant ecclesiastical stained glass was Robert McCausland Limited, so that company was chosen to do the crafting. After several meetings and much thoughtful consideration the group chose two window designs which were meaningful to the history of the Church.

THE OLDHAM WINDOW - East side

Scarborough was a farming region at the turn of the century. This was the trade followed by the Oldhams, thus a **Sheaf of Wheat** was chosen to represent that occupation. This **Grain** is also the fundamental element of the bread that is shared in this sanctuary. The **Bunch of Grapes** flowing toward the **Chalice** represents not only the shared element, but also the outflowing of love that is shared among the worshippers as they meet and participate in service together.

THE THOMSON / McCOWAN WINDOW - West side

The SPIRIT, the **Dove**, gracefully hovers at the apex of this uplifting window. This symbolizes the source of strength of the church. Both the McCowan and the Thomson families served as elders and managers, guarding the spiritual direction of St. Andrew's. The **Lamp of Learning** signifies the knowledge that leads to wisdom - a meaningful sign of the study that is a part of the Learning of the Word. The gathering of the **Fishes** symbolizes the care and concern for the well-being of the congregation.

These windows are dedicated to the Glory of God and are a colourful and inspirational focal point to all who meet to worship in this historical building.

The installation of the Memorial Windows after the restoration of 1990. Two front windows, which had long been sealed and plastered over, were opened again for the placement of the two memorial windows.

*Jean (Oldham) Nauta, Edward Oldham, Rev. Wendell MacNeill,
Bill McAndless (Clerk of Session)
at the Dedication of the "Margaret and Ewart Oldham" Memorial Window (Grapes, Wine and Wheat), Sunday, October 21, 1990, at the front left of the church.*

Stained Glass window dedicated October 21, 1990 in memory of Richard Servos Thomson and Janet and Harold McCowan

Janet, Christie and Ken Campbell, David Thomson, Noelle Thomson and Heather Campbell

Rear: Robert Wakelin, Bob (R.P.) McCowan, Richard Presunka, Bill (W.D.) McCowan, Ethel (Britton) McCowan, Jack (J.R.) McCowan
Second Row: Ann (McCowan) Wakelin, Barbara (McCowan) Presunka, Ruth (McCowan) Dobslaw, Nancy (Weir) McCowan, Beatriz (Ceballos) McCowan, Bruce McCowan
Front Row: Evan Wakelin, Tanya Presunka, Chris Presunka, Traci Thomson, Miranda Thomson, Kim (Midgley) Thomson, Helen (McCowan) Thomson

STEEPLE RESTORATION 1992

Submitted by Ruth Finn

Concern over leaks from the steeple had been expressed over many years. Various methods of repair were explored. Consensus was reached in July of 1992 and a committee was formed. Members of this committee were Alan Leach, David Keith, Robert Watters, Claire Elms, Kathleen Corbett, and Ruth Finn.

As St. Andrew's is a designated historical building, all exterior materials and design must be duplicated. This could be done in various ways, but it was the decision of the committee to use pine tongue-and-groove siding, as was the original. Following receipt of a number of quotations, Heritage Restorations was given the contract. Work commenced in August, 1992 and was completed in September.

The original weather vane was brought to the ground by the steeplejacks and it was found that the years had taken their toll. An iron shop replaced the rusted and bullet-riddled areas to match the original. A large metal ball was spun to replace the wooden one and a smaller one purchased to be placed where one had been originally at the top. The spire was coated with Alumanation - a thick product which would fill small holes and cracks. As the metal cladding (probably zinc and tin) is the original, not too many years ahead we may have to re-cover it.

The siding was applied with the quoined corners, then painted white as the original had been. Some notes of interest are that the lower tower is 10 feet square and the upper one 8 feet square.

When boards were removed from the steeple, it was apparent that the wide interior boards, once the exterior, had been painted white and had quoined corners. Also, large arched shapes were visible on the sides of the tower, probably surrounding a shuttered area.

Total cost, including the extension of the lightning rod system, was $25,800. A government grant was applied for and received in the amount of $3,000.

On February 20, 1995, St. Andrew's received a very well-deserved Heritage Conservation Award from the City of Scarborough. In June, 1995 the church received another award from the City, the Urban Design Award.

Steeple repair during the restoration. The steeple had long been painted a brick colour with a silvery roof. Research suggested that the original steeple had been white, so it was decided to paint the steeple white after repairs were complete.

Inside the steeple during the restoration in 1990.

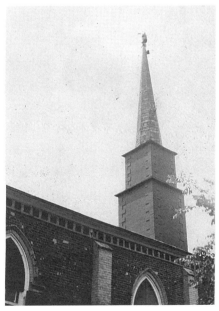

Steeple showing Steeplejack at the top
Probably taken in 1939. Steeple Painter - C.C. Miner
Cost - $50.00 (from Treasurer's Book)

A PROGRESSIVE RECYCLING SOCIETY

Submitted by Bruce McCowan

The stories of the buildings at St. Andrew's parallel the progress of many of Scarborough's nineteenth century farm families.

While many St. Andrew's people in 1833 were still living in a three-room log cabin, they evidently felt that their first manse should be "frame," that is, wooden cladding on a timber structure. For twenty years it was the home of Rev. James George and his family, from the first year of his ministry at St. Andrew's to the last.

The ingenuity of the nineteenth century St. Andrew's farmers shows up in the use and re-use of this building. We can also follow some of the progress of the larger community in the course of these changes.

After the construction of the brick manse in 1853, toward the end of Rev. George's stay, the first manse was used as a Sunday School. Prior to this some classes were conducted in the home of the Minister, while others were probably held in the homes of members of the congregation.

In 1878 the *frame* White Sunday School was built. The First (remember *frame*) Manse was then moved to opposite the brand new Sexton's House for use as the Township Library. When the *brick* Centennial Memorial Library was built in 1896, the First Manse was sold to Robert Thomson for $7.00.

While the First Manse is gone and the Sunday School materials have been recycled for use in cottages, we can be thankful that the 100 year old Library remains, waiting patiently for a new use. In this 1990's era of the "bottom line" and "paying your own way," perhaps St. Andrew's could operate a "Wedding Chapel" in the Centennial Memorial Library.

THE ORIGINAL FRAME CHURCH

Submitted by Bruce McCowan

This very progressive nineteenth century Scottish attitude of "improvement" was reflected in the relatively early decision of the Congregation to replace the original frame church with the present brick building which, as we have seen, was almost extravagant for the place and period. The original 30 foot by 40 foot frame church was situated near the centre of the present burial ground. The following paragraph, written by Mrs. Ross, a daughter of Rev. James George, is valuable for its fairly detailed description of a near-extinct type of early Ontario church building.

The first church as I remember it was frame, with a stair built on the outside to give access to a gallery, added when the congregation grew too large for the ground floor. The church was seated with wooden pews. A long narrow table extended from before the pulpit nearly to the door, a long pew on each side of it; a shorter table and pews were placed across the end of the church on each side of the pulpit. These were the communion tables and pews. The pulpit, a high enclosed place, was reached by a stair. The precentor's desk, directly in front of and lower than the pulpit, was also enclosed.

After the construction of the present church, the original frame church was, according to one story, sold to one of the members for re-use as a farm outbuilding -- as we might have guessed!

THE "OLD" MANSE - 1853

Submitted by Nancy McCowan

A second house was built for the minister, just in time for the arrival of the third, Rev. James Bain. This brick manse was erected in 1853 and it must have been the pride of the congregation when it was finished. Tastes changed and window trim weathered. It was remodeled in 1896.

It is not clear what the remodeling entailed, but perhaps it was at that time that the back kitchen or "Summer Kitchen" was added, apparently for a cost of 149 pounds, 10 shillings and 6 pence. This part consisted of one big room downstairs and probably one big room upstairs. There was a cook stove to use in the summer to keep the heat out of the main part of the house (hence, the term "Summer Kitchen").

The main part of the house was built on the two-storey, center hall plan, as were many houses of that era. The stairs went up the middle with a large kitchen and dining room on one side of the hall and the living room and possibly a study on the other. Upstairs there were originally four bedrooms. No bathrooms existed then as we know them now. They probably bathed in a large metal tub in the kitchen where there was close access to hot water from the cook stove.

The house was built in the last year of Rev. James George's ministry. The church itself was built in 1849 after he had been there for sixteen years. After Rev. George, there was a succession of twelve ministers and their families who made the manse their home. We do not know the size of the various families, but it stands to reason that there were many people who passed through the halls of that building.

Tom Hawthorne, Chairman of the Board of Managers for a time, recalled that Rev. MacLellan had been complaining about the stove in the back kitchen of the manse. He was insisting that it smoked and wanted a new one. One day, at the end of the Church Service, he announced that the problem had to be resolved, and then stalked out.

There was very little money available at the time, so they could not afford to get a new stove. Tom bought a stove from Allen Thomson and had it installed. It turned out that the flue had been too small for the stove and the smoke had not been getting away properly. The Treasurer's book for the period recorded that the "Good Neighbours Club" donated money for a "Stove."

Over the years the Manse needed repairs, new furnaces, plumbing, painting and papering. Wood dries out and shrinks, plaster cracks and mortar falls out from between bricks. During the Depression of the 1930's very few people in Scarborough had enough money to live on, let alone enough to spend on repairs for someone else's house. The two Great Wars saw people expending their efforts on helping to defeat the common enemy.

It was not until 1930 that hydro was installed in the St. Andrew's Church and Manse. Although there was a cistern in the cellar of the house, the only water system would be a handpump in the kitchen which would bring rain water up from the cistern for washing. Drinking water would be pumped at the well outside. It would be only after the installation of hydro that a system for hot and cold running water was possible.

Each time there was a change of ministers, the manse would be empty for a period of time. At the time of the Scarboro Township Sesquicentennial Celebrations (150th Anniversary) on June 29, 30, and July 1, 1946, the manse was unoccupied. The ladies of the church used the empty manse for a display of antiques. The display was arranged by Mrs. T.A. (Ida) Paterson of Agincourt who was quite well-known in the area for her antiques, her many varieties of lilacs and her parrot in the kitchen. Rev. Frank Conkey recalls visiting Mrs. Paterson at her home. After being invited to "sign the visitor's book," he "placed pencil against paper" and discovered that the point was made of rubber and would not write. The parrot cackled. Mrs. Paterson must have played this joke on many visitors.

After the Second World War, many people immigrated to Canada from Holland. The manse was empty following Rev. MacLellan's departure and so it was offered for use by newcomers. One of these families was the Vandermeys (including six children at that time) who lived in the back part. When Rev. Conkey arrived, the yard was covered with boxes of household goods. He was met by Mrs. Vandermey, who was quite upset. They were supposed to move to Markham, but had just been informed by the lawyer, Milne Freeman of Agincourt, that the deal had fallen through, leaving them with nowhere to go. Frank immediately told them to pick up their belongings and return them to the house, and that they could stay there as long as they needed to.

The Church Board told Frank that he could charge them rent if he liked, since the manse was officially his house. However, he made a deal with the Vandermeys that he would have one evening meal a week with them instead of them having to pay rent. This arrangement continued as long as they stayed there. Two of the Vandermey's sons, Nicholas and Kees, went into the ministry, and a daughter, Anne, became a deaconess.

In 1952 St. Andrew's was served by a student minister, Calvin Chambers, who lived in Toronto. The house was unoccupied during these few months. When Rev. Conkey arrived in 1953, the house could be described as being in desperate condition. The floorboards, probably pine, had shrunk and great cracks showed between the boards. Someone joked to Agnes Conkey that she could just sweep the dirt down the cracks. Linoleum was bought for the kitchen floor. The Conkeys bought a grey and green rug for the front room, and the Camerons gave them a rug for the dining room.

The house was very cold in winter, with no storm windows and no heat upstairs. A bathroom had been installed by this time. At least the fixtures had been installed in the corner of one of the big bedrooms. It must have been terribly cold bathing in the winter. Storm windows were eventually put on and a new furnace was purchased.

For part of the time that Mr. Conkey was minister, the F. Uithoven family lived in the back kitchen part of the house. They were a Dutch family who had recently immigrated, two adults and three children, Henni, Autri and Fritz. Mr. and Mrs. Uithoven were the church caretakers for several years. Agnes Conkey remembers Henni coming into her part of the house screaming that there were bats flying around. Agnes does not remember seeing any in her part of the house.

The deterioration of the house was natural due to its age and usage by so many people. One might feel that perhaps the people were uncaring when repairs were not kept up. However, by 1952 the congregation was very small and St. Andrew's was classed as a Mission Charge. There was very little money to spend on the manse. Also, another explanation could be that there were no women on the Board of Managers or the Session at that time. Many men do not realize just what is needed to make a home run smoothly, and so when a request came in for something for the manse, the Board or Session would send it to a Committee. Perhaps some of the farmhouses owned by the committee members were no better than the manse itself. Committees never seem to move quickly.

Destined to be taken down in 1966, the "Old" Manse had faithfully been home to many, perhaps *too many* during its final years. During the April 1962 Ladies' Pot Luck Supper at the manse, something swooped down at Daisy Gardiner, who then promptly called her husband, Alex, the Chairman of the Board of Managers. The exterminators arrived the next day and "the poor bats soon lost their happy home." Kathleen and Rev. MacNeill no longer needed tennis racquets in bed! So the "Old" Manse brings back one or two not-so-fond memories!

The beginning of the end of the Old Manse came in 1964. From the Board of Managers

Report for that year, we learn that:

The bank loan on the Christian Education Building was retired leaving us free to divert our financial endeavours towards the creation of a new manse and the beautification of our grounds. A Committee was appointed to study methods of providing suitable accommodation for our minister.

The Manse Committee reported that one of five choices regarding accommodation for the minister was to renovate the Old Manse for the Minister's use for a total estimated cost of $21,000. The Manse Committee ultimately recommended "that we proceed with the construction of a new manse for the Minister of St. Andrew's, subject to approval by the congregation at the Annual Meeting." The Committee also recommended "that if a new manse is built, provision for a caretaker's residence on the property be made by using the existing manse. Repairs and renovations to the manse would be required as outlined in above under "Renovating the Old Manse"." Unfortunately, the Old Manse was taken down in 1966.

The following year, "Centennial Fever" swept the country and Canadians bounded into a new era of heritage awareness. Had the "bank loan on the Christian Education Building" not been retired so effectively and so quickly, perhaps the Managers might have been bitten by the "history bug" and the old manse might still stand as another permanent Scarborough museum piece.

The Old Manse on its eastern side looking out toward the location of the present-day manse. Wendell MacNeill pretends to dig out tree roots.